The History
of
Godalming Operatic Society

Eddie Powlesland

LOOK FOR THE ENJOYMENT OF

GILBERT AND SULLIVAN

AND FIND IT WITH

GODALMING OPERATIC SOCIETY

Eddie Powlesland   (2012)

i

I wish to dedicate this book to the numerous people who, since 1925, have done so much to establish the Society's highly regarded reputation.

The history of the Society is relevant to what we do now.

The Society and its members have an obligation to maintain, as custodians, this rich and traditional legacy.

President:

Michael Hartnall FCA

Vice Presidents:

Mrs Jean Pratt

and

Robin Wells FRCO GRSM ARCM Hon ARAM

THE HISTORY OF GODALMING OPERATIC SOCIETY

1st Edition October 2012

© 2012 Edwin H. Powlesland and Godalming Operatic Society

Cover design by Piers Plummer

www.godalmingoperatic.org
UK Registered Charity No: 802888

Contents

Acknowledgements

Thank you to the Gilbert & Sullivan Archive for permitting
me to use the background history of each of the operas.

Gilbert & Sullivan Archive website:
http://math.boisestate.edu/gas/

Thank you to the Godalming Music Festival for the additional information
from the History Section of their website.
www.godalmingmusicfestival.org.uk

I would like to express my appreciation to the Society's President,
Michael Hartnall, the Vice-President and Musical Director Robin Wells,
Vice-President Jean Pratt and the former Chairman, Hammy Sparks, for the
information they provided.

I am deeply indebted to Piers Plummer for the excellent work, time and
generous support he has given me in formatting this book. Piers also
created the cover designs.

I would like to thank my wife Pauline, for the immense amount of work
she has done in editing and proof reading this book. Her editorial
comments, meticulous editing and inspirational suggestions have
consistently improved the readability and lucidity of the text. Throughout
the process, Pauline has been a constant source of support and
encouragement. Her help and forbearance have been invaluable to me.

Thank you to Jane Thomas for the final proof reading.

PHOTOGRAPHS

Throughout the book you will see photographs depicting many of our
productions since 1925. The Society is indebted to the people who
have, over the years, donated photographs to add to our archive.

I would also like to acknowledge photographers Peter Sillick and
Jane Thomas who, in more recent years, have enabled the Society
to extend its archive and website gallery.

Preface

Until quite recently I had never thought about writing a book about Godalming Operatic Society. I originally began to look at the possibility of having a page created on our website giving some details of important events in the Society's history. But as I began to gather information, it became quite evident that a website page could not do justice to the Society's long and successful history. Following a discussion with other committee members the idea of a book emerged, so I accepted the challenge.

In the following chapters you will find features about many of the personalities, performers, musicians and others who work behind the scenes for the benefit of the Society – not forgetting their magnificent achievements. The Society's archive has a wealth of information; at the very least I hope that I have, in some way, managed to bring together much of its fascinating history. My sincerest wish was to place on record a fitting acknowledgement to the many people who have done so much over the years. I also felt that special recognition should be made to Betty Moat and to Jean Pratt – stated in Chapter 3.

I wish I could have featured all the people who have done so much to bring the Society to what it is today. But that would have been a challenge too far!

Eddie Powlesland October 2012

SOUVENIR POSTER OF THE MILLENIUM PRODUCTION OF
THE PIRATES OF PENZANCE

Foreword

Michael Hartnall
President of Godalming Operatic Society

This is a book that needed to be written. As the Society approaches its 90th birthday, inevitably even the senior members now only have second-hand memories of the productions before World War Two. We are indebted to Eddie Powlesland for writing this history, thereby capturing the Society's activities and memories before they are lost in the mists of time. Eddie has successfully woven the weft of yesterday with the warp of today, to produce a fascinating book that is not just dry history but a vibrant portrayal of a living Society.

Gilbert and Sullivan created a unique canon of works often called The Savoy Operas. These comic operas remain hugely popular throughout the English speaking world, although it must be admitted that they have never been too successful in translation.

Richard D'Oyly Carte, the talented impresario, was the business partner of Gilbert and Sullivan. He not only built the Savoy Theatre and the Savoy Hotel but he created also the D'Oyly Carte Opera Company that toured, for over 100 years, the Savoy Operas in Britain, the Empire and North America. Eventually, by 1982, touring opera companies became financially unviable and the permanent company closed.

For many decades the amateur societies looked to the D'Oyly Carte Opera Company as the fount of all wisdom on the production of the Savoy Operas. No longer. Today it is the amateur societies that carry the torch for Gilbert and Sullivan. Of course, there are occasional productions of the Savoy Operas mounted by our national companies, but the real activity today is from the strong Gilbert and Sullivan societies.

The Godalming Operatic Society since its inception has been committed to mounting a high quality annual production of one of the Savoy Operas, directed by a professional conductor and director. This basic formula has continued to the present, albeit that there are many more performances now than given in 1925. Today the Society is in robust health. The membership is strong, supported by many patrons and an enthusiastic audience in both Godalming and Leatherhead. Even the finances are in good shape, which is unusual for any opera company.

None of this would be possible were it not for the extraordinary legacy bequeathed to us by our absent friends - Gilbert and Sullivan. Many pages, chapters and books have been written that have attempted to explain why the Savoy Operas were so successful in their own day and why they remain popular today. May I offer my own explanation in one word, a word that is beyond analysis: genius.

Michael Hartnall *August 2012*

THE YEOMEN OF THE GUARD
GODALMING 1925

viii

CHAPTER 1
SETTING THE SCENE.

The first recorded meeting of Godalming Operatic Society took place on 13th October 1924 with Mr G.R. Burgess in the Chair. *Mr and Mrs Burgess* (the Jack Point and Dame Carruthers of their day) who did much to lay the foundations of the Society in its first years together with *Mr H.J. Shindler*, who produced the first show, and *Miss Rose Keen*, who was the Society's accompanist until 1930. *Mr H.D. Coates* was the first treasurer and co-guarantor with Mr Burgess. The first secretary was *Miss D.F. Barnes.*

No doubt, and much before that first meeting in October 1924, local people had been asked about being founder members as either performers, musicians, or to become a member of a group in order to establish the Society and to prepare for the first production. It may be worthwhile pondering for a moment or two to consider the timing of the foundation. It is possible that the timing is associated with the end of the Great War in 1918 and the economic difficulties that quickly followed. So, perhaps, in 1924 people were now ready and had the resources to produce their own entertainment locally. One thing is certain: that since our foundation all those years ago, we have been at the forefront of Godalming's rich musical heritage.

In the following pages you will find much more detail about all of the Society's Gilbert and Sullivan productions and when they were performed, starting with **The Yeomen of the Guard** in 1925.

In 1925 we only gave four performances of **The Yeomen of the Guard.** Since then the number of performances have steadily grown. With the addition of Guildford in 1949 and subsequently Leatherhead in 2004, we now give six performances in Godalming and four in Leatherhead.

It is amazing to think that since 1925 the Society has only had six musical directors. All of them, bar the first one, were from Charterhouse School. Strong links have since been maintained with the school up to the present time. The musical director engages the services of first-rate musicians both professional and some amateur to make up the orchestra for all the G&S productions. They also work closely with the rehearsal accompanists.

The Society's first President was *Mr P.C. Fletcher,* who was a Housemaster at Charterhouse. He was also the Town Mayor at the time of the first production.

In all that time, since 1925, the Society has engaged the services of just 20 producers - 11 of whom were former performers with D'Oyly Carte. At least three of those had performed under the direction of W.S. Gilbert.

Venues for the Society's performances have, over the years, been quite varied but Godalming Borough Hall has been, and still is, the "home" theatre for all the G&S shows. Performances also take place at The Leatherhead Theatre. Other venues have included Charterhouse School, Guildford Technical College, Guildford Civic Hall and even Guildford Cathedral!

Sadly, the annual G&S productions had to cease for the duration of the Second World War. The 1939 production was **H.M.S. Pinafore** with **Trial by Jury.** Productions resumed in 1947 with **The Gondoliers.**

In 1947 members of the Society, including musical director *Arthur Trew*, played a very active role in the establishment of the Godalming Music Festival. Participation by the Society from that first year was quite considerable and we frequently won trophies. Unfortunately, after a change of dates in 1968, the links with Festival became limited. Although our links are less formal now, some of our members do enter for the competitive part of the Festival.

Such is the reputation of the Society that in recent years two of our productions were performed further afield. In 2005 we were invited to perform **Iolanthe** at The International Gilbert and Sullivan Festival in Buxton's beautiful Opera House. In 2007 the production of **Utopia Limited** was performed in Ireland at the Waterford International Festival of Light Opera in the city's historic Theatre Royal. An invitation was extended once again, to perform at the International Festival in Buxton in 2012: this time with **The Pirates of Penzance.**

IOLANTHE 2005, UTOPIA LIMITED 2007 AND THE PIRATES OF PENZANCE 2012

Godalming Operatic Society is not all about Gilbert and Sullivan as there is usually a light hearted Summer Concert in June at the Electric Theatre in Guildford. A different theme or topic is chosen each year for the Summer Concert and on occasions a one act opera is included. In 2008 the concert was held at Godalming Borough Hall and it included the one-act opera **A Frank Affair**, especially written for the Society. A number of special "one off" performances are given by the Society too. On 5th June 2012 a special performance celebrating Her Majesty the Queen's Diamond Jubilee took place. The Diamond Jubilee performance was to have taken place at the Godalming town bandstand; but due to poor weather it was held in the Parish Church of SS Peter & Paul. More information can be found in Chapter 5: "Other Productions and Summer Concerts".

From the early days of planning a production right through to the "final curtain" a great deal of work has to be done. You will find details in Chapter 14: "How it All Works".

Tradition has always been one of the Society's strongest assets and it is important to recognise its rich heritage. Even in this modern day and age microphones are not used at our performances - not that there were any available in 1925! To attend any of the shows means that audiences can enjoy live theatre in its purest form. Although the Society remains true to those traditional roots we have to keep up with the times from the point of view of communication. Email plays a large part in keeping members informed about the Society's activities. Our website also has up to date information too. But more importantly, the website has a wonderful Gallery depicting all our G&S productions, cast lists and orchestra lists. A vast collection of photographs is also included. Other information can also be found on the website.

After much deliberation and consideration, I decided to include representative cast lists only. I estimated that to have included all the cast names for each and every production, it would have produced lists totalling somewhere in the region of 1500 names. You will find included one cast list from each decade representing each of the main G&S operas starting with **The Yeomen of the Guard** in 1925. The only exceptions are that two operas are included for the 1980s: **The Mikado** and **H.M.S. Pinafore** and two from the first decade of this century, **The Grand Duke** and **Utopia Limited**. All the cast lists since 1925, from each of our annual Gilbert and Sullivan productions, can be viewed on our website.

Apart from the cast, many other people have been involved with our G&S productions since 1925. There are the orchestras of course and many more who work behind the scenes for the Society each year. By the time we bring each of our G&S productions to the stage well over 100 people will have been involved. With fewer performances in the early days that number would have probably been smaller. In 2013 we shall be presenting our 83rd full production.

As we begin our journey from first production in 1925 right through to the present day, you will see references to our musical directors and producers; some of our producers had previously performed with D'Oyly Carte. References are also made to personalities and performers. Where such named references are made either in this chapter or in the pages dedicated to the operas they will appear *in italic*. It will indicate that more details about the individual will be found in the appropriate chapter.

Much has been written about Gilbert and Sullivan but as a society so devoted to their works, I think it is important to include a short chapter about the famous pair. It is also worth mentioning that all the G&S operas (including **Trial by Jury**) are generally referred to as the Savoy Operas. In a strict sense however, the first true Savoy Opera was **Patience** in 1881.

It is perhaps interesting to note that apparently **The Grand Duke,** until 2012, had not been performed professionally in England fully staged and with an orchestra since its original production over 100 years ago. As an amateur society we were pleased to perform **The Grand Duke** for the first time in 2001. And, as with all our G&S productions, it was fully staged with an orchestra.

CHAPTER 2
GILBERT AND SULLIVAN

William Schwenck Gilbert   (1836 - 1911)

William Schwenck Gilbert made a huge contribution to making the Savoy operas what they are — witty, dry, romantic, subversive, nonsensical and very funny. He directed the first productions and often contributed towards the costume and set designs. He also achieved much else — writing some of the funniest and most scandalous comedies of his day, writing and illustrating those grotesque masterpieces the Bab Ballads, and building London's Garrick Theatre, amongst other things. He was knighted in 1907.

Arthur Seymour Sullivan   (1842 – 1900)

Gilbert once described Arthur Sullivan as "incomparably the greatest English musician of the age." Besides contributing witty operatic parodies and a string of effervescent melodies to the Savoy operas, he wrote, amongst other works, cantatas, oratorios, concert overtures, incidental music to plays, numerous songs and a grand opera. He was the conductor of the Leeds Festival for almost 20 years, a friend of Royalty and a keen follower of the turf. He was knighted in 1883.

Although this chapter is devoted to Gilbert and Sullivan, we must also remember the role that Richard D'Oyly Carte played in bringing the pair together, and the establishment of the Savoy Operas. His role was invaluable in setting the foundation of such rich and lasting tradition. Although the relationship between all three gentlemen was at times strained, at the end of the day, all that can be said is that their continuing legacy is something that Godalming Operatic Society is proud of.

CHAPTER 3
A SPECIAL RECOGNITION

There are two people who I believe deserve special recognition for their contribution to Godalming Operatic Society over many years. They are Betty Moat and Jean Pratt.

Betty Moat BA LGSM

The daughter of founder members of the Society, Mr & Mrs C.E. Moat, Betty joined the Society in 1938 and played her first principal role, Fiametta, in **The Gondoliers** in 1947.

Betty was Secretary of the Society for 29 years. Following her retirement from office in 1999 she was appointed President – a post she held until her death in 2004. During her years as Secretary Betty supported six Chairmen, all of whom were wholly reliant on her support and commitment. Untiring in her efforts, she really was the Pooh-Bah of the Society! One of the extra tasks she took on, and which she particularly enjoyed, was acting as compère for our Summer Concerts in which she would write introductory notes on all the items being performed.

It is really not possible to relate in these few lines just how much Betty did for the Society over the years; but it is true to say that no-one can, or will ever, do more.

In writing this book I found the special article written by Betty for the Savoyard magazine at the time of our Golden Jubilee in 1975 of immense help.

Jean Pratt (née Gaff) Vice-President.

Joining the Society in 1951, Jean's first performance was as Sacharissa in **Princess Ida** in 1952, after which she went on to play many leading roles. She sang professionally for two years before returning to the Society in 1966.   In 1977 Jean married Keith Pratt, who was also a principal in many of our productions. He was Chairman of the Society from 1989 to 1994.

**Jean, as Elsie Maynard, in
THE YEOMEN OF THE GUARD 1972**

It is without doubt that Jean's biggest contribution to the Society was as a singer. Jean was extremely accomplished on stage and is probably one of the best singers the Society has ever had. She was our principal soprano for many years before moving to some of the soubrette roles and eventually to contralto roles.

Appointed as Honorary Patrons' Secretary in 1994, Jean was subsequently appointed Honorary Secretary of the Society in 1998, following Betty's retirement. As part of her role as Secretary, Jean has been very much involved in the management of all our rehearsals and during performances standing in the wings as our "prompter". She was also editor of the Society's Newsletter "The Peeper" from 1984 until 2009.

In 2012 Jean, already a life member, decided to step down as our Honorary Secretary. At the 2012 Annual General Meeting Michael Hartnall, our President, paid tribute to her long and loyal service.   In recognition of this Jean was presented with an engraved crystal rose bowl. On a memorable evening it was with unanimous approval, and to the delight of all in attendance, that Jean should be appointed Vice-President of the Society.

Although Jean has stepped down from her Honorary Secretary role, she remains as custodian of the Society's superb archive. In writing this book I was very grateful to Jean for all her guidance, support, encouragement and information. I also enjoyed listening to many interesting anecdotes as well! Jean has such an in depth knowledge of the Society and I know there are many more stories about events that have taken place over the years. I do hope that throughout this book I have been able to encapsulate, and place on record, many of those stories. In addition, you will find an amusing anecdote relating to Jean in Chapter 12: "The Godalming Music Festival".

Once again it is impossible to relate how much Jean has done for the Society over a great number of years. All I can add, is that I hope that this special recognition chapter will serve as a testament to the outstanding accomplishments and dedication given to the Society by both Betty and Jean.

CHAPTER 4
THE OPERAS 1925 to 2012

THE YEOMEN OF THE GUARD

The Yeomen of the Guard, or The Merryman and His Maid, opened on 3rd October 1888 at the Savoy Theatre and ran for 423 performances. The darkest of the Gilbert and Sullivan operas, "Yeomen" ends with a broken-hearted main character and at least two reluctant engagements, rather than the usual armful of marriages. However, Gilbert's "pointed" satire and punning one-liners abound, there are plenty of topsy-turvy plot complications. Many people believe that the score is Sullivan's finest. Indeed, some enjoy **Yeomen,** particularly because of its ever-changing emotional balance of joy and despair, love and sacrifice.

The Society's first ever performance was on Thursday, 19th February 1925. The curtains opened at The Borough Hall, Godalming to reveal Phoebe, played by *Violet Streeter,* at her spinning wheel. The producer was *Mr Herbert Shindler* and the musical director was *Dr A. A. Mackintosh.* There were just four performances of this first production.

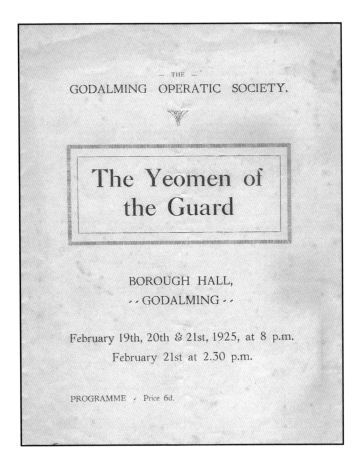

7

1925 DRAMATIS PERSONÆ
"THE YEOMEN OF THE GUARD"

Sir Richard Cholmondeley	Mr . J.H. Taylor
Colonel Fairfax	Mr. F. Deane-Ransome
Sergeant Meryll	Mr . W. Bennett
Leonard Meryll	Rev. D. Hiam
Jack Point	Mr. G.R Burgess
Wilfred Shadbolt	Mr. G.F. Barrington
The Headsman	Rev. F.S. Colson
First Yeoman	Mr. C.E. Moat
Second Yeoman	Capt. G.M. Baker
First Citizen	Mr. G.F. Arthur
Second Citizen	Mr. A. Faulconbridge
Elsie Maynard	Miss S. Rothwell
Phoebe Meryll	Miss V. Streeter
Dame Carruthers	Mrs. G.R Burgess
Kate	Mrs. Williams

Chorus of Yeomen of the Guard, Citizens etc:
Messrs. A.H. Brownrigg, Holmes, Locke, Mackintosh, H. W. Pointer,
H.W. Stevens, J.S. Spring.

Mesdames Brownrigg, Hurman, Moat, C. Randall, A. Rothwell and
W. Rothwell, the Misses Barnes, Beale, L. Debenham, Edwards, Enticknap,
Glanister , Greenfield, Hartfree, Martin, Markwick, Parrott, Pointer, Peachey,
Robertson, Thornton, Wells, White, Wynn.

THE YEOMEN OF THE GUARD 1925

The Yeomen of the Guard was next performed in 1931 and was produced by *Hugh Enes* and
Tessa Blackmore with musical direction by *Arthur Trew.* It would be another 20 years before
we performed **Yeomen** for the third time when, in 1951, the producer was *C. William Morgan*
with musical direction by *Arthur Trew. C. William Morgan* was also the producer on the next

8

occasion in 1961 with *David Stone* as musical director. The 1972 production saw *Leonard Osborn* as producer and *Robin Wells,* now in his second year, as musical director.

THE YEOMEN OF THE GUARD 1951

The 1980 and 1989 productions saw *Cynthia Morey* and *Meston Reid* respectively as producers, with *Robin Wells* as musical director. There were no performances at the Borough Hall in 1980 due to building renovation.

THE YEOMEN OF THE GUARD 1980

Paul Weakley, who had performed with D'Oyly Carte played the part of Colonel Fairfax in the 1999 production. *Michael Harding* was the producer with musical direction by *Robin Wells.*

Our most recent production of **Yeomen** was in 2010, *Pat O'Connell* was the producer and *Robin Wells*, once again, was the musical director.

THE YEOMEN OF THE GUARD 2010

It was at the time of the 2010 production when *Robin Wells* celebrated his 40th year with the Society as musical director. On the final evening of the Godalming performances Robin was presented with a commemorative card by *Michael Hartnall*, our President. The card featured front cover copies of the programmes of all the G&S productions that Robin had directed for us.

PRESENTATION TO ROBIN WELLS

10

PRINCESS IDA

Princess Ida, or **Castle Adamant,** opened on 5th January 1884 at the Savoy Theatre and ran for 246 performances. It is the only three act Gilbert and Sullivan opera and the only one with dialogue in blank verse. This is because Gilbert based his libretto on his earlier play *The Princess* which, in turn, he described as "a perversion" of Tennyson's poem of the same name. It was produced between **Iolanthe** and **The Mikado** when its creators were at the height of their powers. The score is Sullivan at his best and some people consider that Gilbert's libretto contains some of his funniest lines.

Our production of **Princess Ida** in 1926 saw the arrival of our first producer with D'Oyly Carte connections: *Hugh Enes Blackmore.* He and his wife *Tessa* had a long association with the Society. *Arthur Trew* made his debut as musical director in 1926. The 1935 stage direction was carried out by the *Blackmores* and *Arthur Trew* was the musical director.

GODALMING
OPERATIC
SOCIETY

PRESENT . .

GILBERT & SULLIVAN'S

"Princess Ida"

Or, CASTLE ADAMANT

(By permission of R. D'Oyly Carte, Esq.)

THE BOROUGH HALL
Feb. 6th, 7th, 8th & 9th
1935   Price 6d.

G. S. SKELTON, PRINTER, GODALMING.

1935 DRAMATIS PERSONÆ
"PRINCESS IDA"

King Hildebrand	Kenneth F. Swayne
Hilarion	Charles Brown
Cyril	Philip C. Fletcher
Florian	William Bennett
King Gama	Kenneth Roberts
Arac	John W. Smith
Guron	Harry W. Stevens
Scynthius	Herbert Thatcher
Princess Ida	Mrs Cyril Randall
Lady Blanche	Miss Madge Matthews
Lady Psyche	Miss Winifred Woodstock
Melissa	Miss Violet Streeter
Sacharissa	Miss Kathleen Beale
Chloe	Miss Kathleen Bowyer
Ada	Miss Winifred N. Pilcher

Chorus of Soldiers, Courtiers, Girl Graduates, Daughters of the Plough etc:
Mrs C.E. Hart, Miss G. Brunning, Miss E.M. Mobbs, Miss E.M. Wells,
Mrs F.S. Porter, Miss C. Dracott, Miss P.D. Perry, Miss K. Bullen, Mrs C.J. Pugsley,
Miss L. Giles, Miss P.M. Swayne, Miss G. Pridgeon, Miss B. Armstrong,
Miss P.W. W. Grover, Miss H.R. Titcomb, Miss V. Wildie.

C.E. Bateman, R.E. Gates, W.J. Lee, A.P. Squire, J.C. Bristow, H. Hellier, J.H. Parrott,
W.G.M. Swayne, W.H. Caldwell, W.B. Hoare, C.A. Pridgeon.

PRINCESS IDA 1926

Princess Ida was performed again in 1952. The producer was *C. William Morgan* and musical direction once again by *Arthur Trew.* The performance scheduled for 15th February 1952 was cancelled, as this was the day of the funeral of H.M. King George VI.

In 1960 *C. William Morgan* took care of stage direction with *David Stone* as musical director. The producer in 1971 was *Leonard Osborn* and *Robin Wells* made his debut as musical director. Our 1982 producer was *Doris Relph* and *Robin Wells* was the musical director.

PRINCESS IDA 1960

Meston Reid was producer in 1992 with *Robin Wells* as musical director. *Hammy Sparks* took a break from performing in order to direct our 2003 production, with *Robin Wells* as musical director.

PRINCESS IDA 1992 AND 2003

THE GONDOLIERS

The Gondoliers, or **The King of Barataria**, was the 12th opera written by Gilbert and Sullivan. Opening on 7th December 1889 at the Savoy Theatre, **The Gondoliers** ran for 554 performances and was the last of the G&S operas that would achieve wide popularity. Its lilting score has, perhaps, the most sparkling and tuneful music.

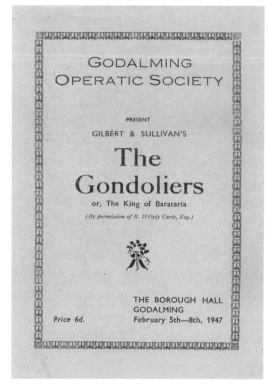

THE GONDOLIERS 1927

Our first production of **The Gondoliers** in 1927 was under the direction of *Hugh Enes Blackmore,* now assisted by his wife *Tessa (née Snelson),* who had also performed with D'Oyly Carte. Musical direction was by *Arthur Trew.* We next performed the opera in 1933 and direction this time was again by *Mr Blackmore* and *Tessa. Arthur Trew* was musical director.

Following the end of the Second World War we resumed our productions in 1947 with **The Gondoliers.** The producer was *Clara Dow* who had also performed with D'Oyly Carte. Miss Dow was described in the programme as "Late Prima Donna The D'Oyly Carte Opera Company". Musical director once again was **Arthur Trew. Betty Moat,** who had a long association with Society, performed her first principal role as Fiametta in this production. Not to help matters the winter of 1947 was particularly harsh; nevertheless people queued in the snow to obtain tickets and a total sell-out was achieved.

1947 DRAMATIS PERSONÆ
"THE GONDOLIERS"

The Duke of Plaza-Toro	Frank Broadbent
Luiz	William Bennett
Don Alhambra del Bolero	Rolf Whicker
Marco Palmieri	Charles Brown
Giuseppe Palmieri	Kenneth Roberts
Antonio	Ian C. Hamilton
Francesco	Charles Bateman
Giorgio	William Crane
Annibale	Geoffrey Brown
The Duchess of Plaza-Toro	Mrs. K. Roberts
Casilda	Miss Edith Gooder
Gianetta	Mrs. R.F. Raper
Tessa	Miss Pamela Blofeld
Fiametta	Miss Betty Moat
Vittoria	Miss Joan Marshall
Giulia	Miss Teresa Honess
Inez	Mrs. W.J. Lee

Ladies of the Chorus:
Miss M. Bedford, Miss M. Berry, Mrs S.V. Bierton, Miss C. Boshier, Miss H. Dean, Miss B. Enticknap, Mrs A.E. Funnell, Miss U. Gregory, Miss P. Hewer, Miss R.J. Hollowell, Mrs W.J. Lee, Mrs C.J. Pugsley, Miss E. Skelton, Miss C. Streeter, Miss H.R Titcomb, Miss M.E. Turton.

Gentlemen of the Chorus:
G.L. Brignall, G. Cooper, R.W. Frost, S. Heller, H. W. Hellier, H.M. James, W.J. Lee, J.C. Leonard, J.W. Smith, A.P. Squire.

THE GONDOLIERS 1947

15

Arthur Trew was musical director for our 1954 production too, with *C. William Morgan* as the producer. Mr Morgan also directed the 1962 production with musical direction by *David Stone.*

Leonard Osborn, a fine tenor who performed extensively with D'Oyly Carte, directed the 1969 production with *George Draper* as musical director. *Michael Harding* directed the 1979 production and *Robin Wells* was musical director – now in his ninth year with the Society. *Meston Reid* directed the 1991 production with *Robin Wells* as musical director.

THE GONDOLIERS 1979

Director for the 2002 production was again *Michael Harding*. This time, owing to illness, he was assisted by *Paul Weakley*, who also performed in the production as Marco Palmieri. *Robin Wells* was musical director.

THE GONDOLIERS 2002

16

THE PIRATES OF PENZANCE

After the sensational success of **H.M.S. Pinafore** many American performing companies presented unauthorized versions of that opera. Gilbert, Sullivan and Carte decided to prevent that from happening again by presenting official versions of their next opera **The Pirates of Penzance,** or **The Slave of Duty,** simultaneously in England and America. The opera premiered on 31st December 1879 at the Fifth Avenue Theatre in New York with Sullivan conducting; but a single performance had been given on the previous day at the Royal Bijou Theatre, Paignton, England, to secure the British copyright. Finally, the opera opened on 3rd April 1880 at the Opéra Comique in London. It ran for 363 performances, having already been played successfully for over three months in New York.

The Society's first performance of **The Pirates of Penzance** was in 1928. The producer was *Herbert Shindler* who also played the part of the Major General. *Arthur Trew* was musical director.

THE PIRATES OF PENZANCE 1928

In 1936 we performed a double bill of **Pirates** and the brilliant **Cox and Box.** Once again the *Blackmores* and *Arthur Trew* directed both shows.

A further 23 years elapsed before we performed **Pirates** again – this time, in 1959, with producer *C. William Morgan* and *David Stone* as musical director. The 1970 production was directed by *Leonard Osborn* with *George Draper* as musical director.

THE PIRATES OF PENZANCE 1959

1981 was quite an eventful year. **Pirates** was the main production and it was combined with **The Zoo**. The producer was *Cynthia Morey* with *Robin Wells* as musical director. There is more information about other events in 1981 in Chapter 5 "Other Productions". A double bill was also performed in 1990: this time with **Cox and Box**. *Meston Reid* was producer and *Robin Wells* was musical director.

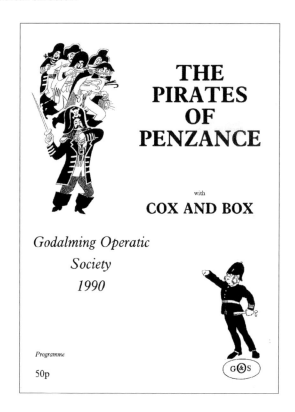

1990 DRAMATIS PERSONÆ
"THE PIRATES OF PENZANCE"

Major Gen. Stanley	David Billett
The Pirate King	Hammy Sparks
Samuel	Nigel Pinkney
Frederic	Myles Harfield
Sergeant of Police	Michael Harding
Mabel	Judy Spooner
Edith	Yvette Pinkney
Kate	Jane Bryant
Isobel	Jacky Tivers
Ruth	Jennifer Simpson

General Stanley's Daughters:
Susannah Barnby, Sue Billett, Jane Currie, Debra Freeman,Pam Hiorns, Barbara Hubble, Julie Kitchen, Karen Lyon, Alison McKay, Heather Parker, Jill Read, Jenny Robbins, Sheila Rowell, Linda Scanlon, Anne Thomas, Jill Tickner, Sue Tilling, Lorna Whike.

Pirates & Policemen:
Ambrose Barber, Ray Bardsley, Tom Briggs, David Burchell, Alistair Bywater, Harry Evans, Peter Gardner, John Mackney, Roger Marjoribanks, Denis O'Donoghue, Nigel Petrie, Anthony Read, John Reid, Michael Scanlon, Shaun Steele.

THE PIRATES OF PENZANCE 1990

Pirates was performed again in 2000 with *Michael Harding* as producer and *Robin Wells* as musical director.

Our 2012 outing of **Pirates** has an extra special feature to add. In addition to our Godalming and Leatherhead performances, an invitation was extended to the Society to perform at The International Gilbert and Sullivan Festival in Buxton's magnificent Opera House on 15th August. The producer was *Pat O'Connell* with *Robin Wells* as musical director.

THE PIRATES OF PENZANCE 2012: FIRST AND SECOND ACTS

IOLANTHE

Iolanthe, or **The Peer and the Peri**, opened at the Savoy Theatre on 25th November 1882 – three nights after the final performance of Patience at the same theatre. It ran for 398 performances.

Gilbert had taken pot shots at the aristocracy before; but in this "fairy opera," the House of Lords is lampooned as a bastion of the ineffective, privileged and dim-witted. The political party system and other institutions also come in for a dose of satire. Yet, both author and composer managed to couch the criticism among such bouncy, amiable absurdities that it is all received as good fun.

Both Gilbert and Sullivan were at the height of their creative powers in 1882 and many people feel that **Iolanthe**, their seventh work together, is the most perfect of their collaborations.

Iolanthe has some extra significance for the Society: in 2005 we were invited to take the production to the International Gilbert and Sullivan Festival in Buxton. Performing in Frank Matcham's magnificent Opera House was a wonderful experience. The producer in 2005 was *Mark Woolgar* and *Robin Wells* was musical director. A great deal of preparation was needed in order to coordinate arrangements for this special performance.

Although the 2005 production was particularly significant, we have to look back to 1929 for our first performance of **Iolanthe**, which was in the capable hands of the *Blackmores* and *Arthur Trew*.

IOLANTHE 1929 AND 1949

21

1976 DRAMATIS PERSONÆ
"IOLANTHE"

The Lord Chancellor	Keith Pratt
Earl of Mountararat	Michael Harding
Earl Tolloller	John Weeks
Private Willis	Bob Martin
Strephon	Adrian Thompson
Queen of the Fairies	Sheila Harman
Iolanthe	Jean Gaff
Celia	Janet Thomson
Leila	Anne Grey
Fleta	Andrea Brabyn
Phyllis	Margaret Bicknell

Chorus of Fairies:
Ann Arnold, Frances Boddy, Yvonne Budd, Pippa Cox, Mary Crockett, Gwen Eyles, Sylvia Gatehouse, Susan Hilborne, Pam Hiorns, Catherine King, Barbara Morgan, Sara Morgan, Lorna Nicholson, Anne Phillips, Jill Rosser, Barbara Simm, Gill Tribe.

Chorus of Dukes, Marquises, Earls, Viscounts and Barons:
Chris Baker, Ambrose Barber, Gerald Bartlett, Frank Bicknell, Charles Brown, Robert Brown, Michael Daniel, Hugh Draper, Arthur Frogley, Frank Greaves, Wilf Hall, Fred Jeffery, Stephen Ladd, John Mackney, Ray Morgan, Keith Neeve, Hamilton Sparks, Brian Waterhouse.

Lord Chancellor's Trainbearer - John Sherlock.

THE GODALMING OPERATIC SOCIETY

present

IOLANTHE

* * *

by W. S. Gilbert and Arthur Sullivan

February-March 1976 — Programme 10p

In 1949 ***Leo Sheffield,*** who had performed with D'Oyly Carte, directed the production with ***Arthur Trew*** as musical director. The year also saw, for the first time, the Society reaching a wider audience. On Saturday 26th February two performances were given at Guildford Technical College, with the aim of raising funds for Farncombe Church.

Iolanthe was performed again in 1957 with ***C. William Morgan*** as producer and ***Arthur Trew*** in his last appearance as musical director.

In 1967 ***William Llewellyn*** was musical director with ***Geoffrey Ford*** as producer and ***Robin Wells*** as chorus master. By the time of our 1976 production ***Robin Wells*** was well established as our musical director. He was joined again by ***Leonard Osborn*** as producer.

IOLANTHE 1976

Michael Harding directed the 1985 production with *Robin Wells* as musical director. There were no performances at the Borough Hall in 1985 due to building renovation.

Robin Wells was also the musical director in 1995 with *Carole Mudie* as producer.

IOLANTHE 1995

THE MIKADO

The Mikado or, **The Town of Titipu**, is one of the most popular Gilbert and Sullivan operas and arguably the most popular opera ever written. This opera has delighted audiences for more than a century and has spawned a number of imitations. But none were nearly as good as the original, which represented both Gilbert and Sullivan at the height of their creative powers.

THE MIKADO 1930

Our first production of **The Mikado** was in 1930 with the *Blackmores* as producers and *Arthur Trew* as musical director. They also directed the 1937 production.

Clara Dow directed the 1948 production with *Arthur Trew* as musical director. *B.W. "Bertie" Holmes* (who was formerly with D'Oyly Carte) directed the 1956 production with *Arthur Trew* as musical director. *C. William Morgan* directed the 1963 production and for the first time *William Llewellyn* was musical director.

1974 saw *Leonard Osborn* as producer with *Robin Wells* as musical director. That was also the year that we first performed at the Guildford Civic Hall.

MIKADO 1963 - CARD SCHOOL

Michael Harding, producer, and *Robin Wells,* musical director, were in charge of the 1983 production.

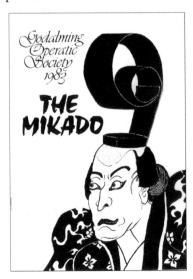

THE MIKADO 1983

The ever popular **The Mikado** was performed again in 1993 with *Robin Wells* as musical director and *Meston Reid* as producer.

THE MIKADO 1993

Apart from Godalming Borough Hall, pastures new beckoned in 2004. After the closure of the Guildford Civic Hall a new second venue was sought. This brought us and **The Mikado** to what is now our "second" home: The Leatherhead Theatre. Many will remember this as the Thorndike Theatre. *Mark Woolgar* was producer and *Robin Wells* was musical director.

PATIENCE

The sixth G&S collaboration was **Patience, or Bunthorne's Bride. Patience** opened on 23rd April 1881 at the Opéra Comique and ran for 578 performances. On 10th October 1881 **Patience** moved to the Savoy - D'Oyly Carte's new theatre – the first theatre in the world to be lit entirely by electric light.

Patience satirises the "aesthetic craze" of the 1870s and 1880s when the output of poets, composers, painters and designers of all kinds was indeed prolific — but, some argued, empty and self-indulgent. This artistic movement was popular; the fact that it was easy to ridicule as a meaningless fad made **Patience** a big hit.

PATIENCE 1932

Patience was first performed by the Society in 1932 and then again in 1938. *Arthur Trew* was musical director and stage direction was by the *Blackmores* on both occasions.

C. William Morgan directed the 1953 and 1964 productions with *Arthur Trew* as musical director in 1953 and *William Llewellyn* in 1964. The 1973 production was directed by *Leonard Osborn* with *Robin Wells as* musical director.

PATIENCE 1973

In 1981 a special concert version of **Patience** was performed in Godalming to celebrate the centenary of the town being the first in the world to have a public electricity supply. More information about this event can be found in Chapter 5: "Our Other Productions".

We next performed the opera in 1987 with *Michael Harding* directing and *Robin Wells* as musical director. The same duo also directed the 1998 production. Former D'Oyly Carte member *Paul Weakley* played the part of the Lieut. The Duke of Dunstable.

PATIENCE 1998

Our 2011 production was directed by *Pat O'Connell* with *Robin Wells* as musical director. The National Operatic and Dramatic Association (NODA) awarded us the "Accolade of Excellence" for our district for this production.

ROBIN WELLS, HAMMY SPARKS AND PAT O'CONNELL WITH THE NODA AWARD

2011 DRAMATIS PERSONÆ
"PATIENCE"

Colonel Calverley	Lee Power
Major Murgatroyd	Sam Barrett
Lieut. The Duke of Dunstable	Jeremy Bourne
Reginald Bunthorne	Simon Cakebread
Archibald Grosvenor	Richard Arthur
Mr Bunthorne's Solicitor	Sue Starbuck
The Lady Angela	Alexandra Lawrence
The Lady Saphir	Ruth Parr
The Lady Ella	Katie Wood
The Lady Jane	Nora Price
Patience	Jenny Sanders

Chorus of Rapturous Maidens:
Sue Barrett, Wendy Bicknell, Katherine Chevis, Charlotte Choi, Rosie Clarke, Margaret Cox, Hannah Crutcher, Claire Don, Chris Howard, Janet Hughes, Sheila Knight, Gillian Lucas, Helen McEvoy, Elaine McGee, Joan Robinson, Barbara Saunders, Linda Scanlon.

Chorus of Officers of Dragoon Guards:
Kai Choi, Harry Evans, Jeff Holliday, David Hughes, Alan Knight, Antony Lucas, Peter Lucas, Peter Melville, Nathan Morley, Piers Plummer, Michael Scanlon, Hammy Sparks, Paul Tickner.

PATIENCE 2011

29

RUDDIGORE

Ruddigore, or **The Witch's Curse,** was the 10th collaboration between Gilbert and Sullivan. The "supernatural opera" opened on January 21, 1887 at the Savoy Theatre and ran for 288 performances. It was not revived until 1920 when it was substantially cut and provided with a new overture arranged by Geoffrey Toye.

The opera is a parody of the stock melodrama — the villain who carries off the maiden; the priggishly good-mannered, poor-but-virtuous-heroine; the hero in disguise, and his faithful old retainer who dreams of their former glory days; the snake in the grass who claims to be following his heart; the wild, mad girl; the swagger of fire-eating patriotism; ghosts coming to life to enforce a curse; and so forth. But, as one critic noted, Gilbert turns the moral absolutes of melodrama upside down: Good becomes bad, bad becomes good; and heroes take the easy way out.

Our 1934 production was directed by the *Blackmores* and *Arthur Trew* was musical director. It would be another 16 years before we performed **Ruddigore** again, this time in 1950 with *Clara Dow* directing and *Arthur Trew* as musical director.

RUDDIGORE 1934

1958 DRAMATIS PERSONÆ
"RUDDIGORE"

Sir Ruthven Murgatroyd	David Clarke
Richard Dauntless	John Rowe
Sir Despard Murgatroyd	John Daykin
Old Adam Goodheart	Frederick Jeffery
Sir Roderic Murgatroyd	Kenneth Roberts
Rose Maybud	Miss Jean Gaff
Mad Margaret	Miss Shirley Springate
Dame Hannah	Mrs. Kenneth Roberts
Zorah	Miss Shirley Butters
Ruth	Miss Christine Streeter

Ladies of the Chorus:
Mrs K.A. Bird, Miss V.J. Brown, Miss J.A. Courtnell, Mrs J.R Daykin,
Miss E.A. Edwards, Miss P.M. French, Miss H.D. Hollis, Miss H. Hydes,
Miss S.A. Jones, Miss M. Mann, Miss B.M. Richardson, Miss M.D. Richardson,
Miss E.J. Sommerfield, Miss J.G. Tomlinson, Mrs D.R. Western.

Gentlemen of the Chorus:
S.F. Beswick, K.A. Bird, R.C. Brown, C. W. Cooper, J.W. Cozens,W. Crane,E.T. Denty,
D. Ellis, R.W. Frost, F.R Greaves, J.H. Hammond, W.S. Rennison, E.G. Venton,
A.L. Wastie,V.F. Woodward.

The 1958 production saw *C. William Morgan* as producer and *David Stone* as musical director.

RUDDIGORE 1958

In 1965 *William Llewellyn* was our musical director and the producer was *Geoffrey Ford*. *Leonard Osborn* directed the 1975 production and *Robin Wells* was musical director. The 1986 production saw *Michael Harding* directing with *Robin Wells* as musical director.

RUDDIGORE 1965

Another former D'Oyly Carte principal *James Conroy-Ward* directed the 1996 production with *Robin Wells* as musical director.

Pat O'Connell (now in his second year with the Society) directed the 2008 production and *Robin Wells* was musical director.

RUDDIGORE 2008

H.M.S. PINAFORE

The fourth collaboration between Gilbert & Sullivan was their first blockbuster hit: **H.M.S. Pinafore**, or **The Lass That Loved a Sailor**. The opera opened on 28th May 1878 at the Opéra Comique. It ran for 571 performances and became a huge fad in England, and also in America, being copied illegally by dozens of performing companies in the USA, as well as being presented there by Gilbert, Sullivan and Carte. **H.M.S. Pinafore** is among the most popular Gilbert and Sullivan operas: perhaps because of its infectious tunes and generally well-constructed libretto.

We performed **H.M.S. Pinafore** for the first time in 1939 when the production was combined with **Trial by Jury**. This was the last production directed for us by the *Blackmores*. *Arthur Trew* was musical director. *Arthur Trew* was again musical director for the 1955 production with *C. William Morgan* as producer.

H.M.S. PINAFORE 1939

Both *William Llewellyn*, musical director, and *Geoffrey Ford*, producer, bowed out after the 1968 production. Chorus director for that year was *Christine Streeter*.

In 1978 the production was again combined with **Trial by Jury**. *Michael Harding* was producer and *Robin Wells* musical director. *Meston Reid* (formerly a D'Oyly Carte principal) directed the 1988 production, which was again combined with **Trial by Jury**. *Robin Wells* was musical director.

H.M.S PINAFORE 1968

1988 DRAMATIS PERSONÆ
"H.M.S. PINAFORE"

The Rt.Hon. Sir Joseph Porter	Nic Wilson
Captain Corcoran	Simon Wilson
Ralph Rackstraw	Tom Briggs
Dick Deadeye	Hammy Sparks
Bill Bobstay	David Billett
Bob Becket	Denis O'Donoghue
Josephine	Fiammetta Doria
Hebe	Nicki Street
Little Buttercup	Jennifer Simpson

Ladies of the Chorus:
Sue Billett, Helen Brudenell-Pride, Jane Currie, Pam Hiorns, Barbara Hubble, Clare Mackney, Alison McKay, Heather Parker, Jacqui Pearson, Susannah Richards, Jenny Robbins, Sheila Rowell, Linda Scanlon, Sheila Smith, Anne Thomas, Jill Tickner , Sue Tilling, Jacky Tivers.

Gentlemen of the Chorus:
Chris Baker, Ambrose Barber, Hugh Draper, Harry Evans, Arthur Frogley, Peter Gardner, Julian Hubble, John Mackney, Geoff Mussett, John Reid, Michael Scanlon, Shaun Steele.

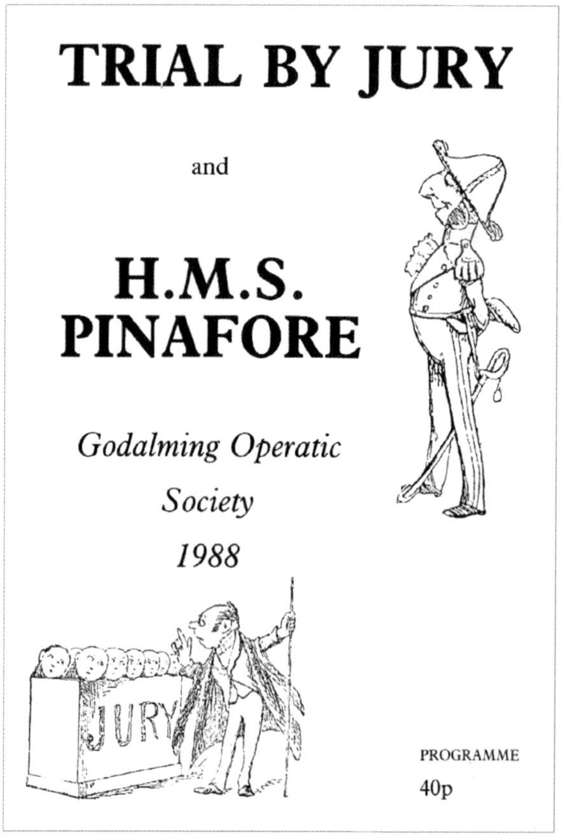

TRIAL BY JURY

and

H.M.S. PINAFORE

Godalming Operatic

Society

1988

PROGRAMME

40p

34

H.M.S PINAFORE 1988

The **Trial by Jury** combination also took place in 1997 with *Michael Harding* directing and *Robin Wells* as musical director. *Paul Weakley* played the part of Ralph Rackstraw. In 2009 *Pat O'Connell* directed and *Robin Wells* was musical director.

H.M.S PINAFORE 1997

THE SORCERER

After the early and resounding success of their one-act opera **Trial by Jury** in 1875, Gilbert and Sullivan, and their producer Richard D'Oyly Carte, decided to produce a full-length work. Gilbert expanded on one of his earlier writings, based on a favourite operatic theme, to create a plot about a magic love potion that would result in everyone falling in love with the wrong partner.

The Sorcerer was first produced at the Opéra Comique – a charming little theatre in the Strand – on 17th November 1877. The original run of the piece was a successful 178 performances. This encouraged Gilbert and Sullivan to continue to collaborate, ultimately leading to their next piece: **H.M.S. Pinafore**. And the rest is history.

It was 1966 before we performed **The Sorcerer** for the first time. We would have liked to have performed **The Sorcerer** a lot earlier; but we were subject to a certain constraint. Permission had to be sought from D'Oyly Carte right up until 1961 to perform the G&S operas. There was, however, a stipulation that to perform **The Sorcerer** the stage had to have a trap door (the stage at Godalming Borough Hall does not have one). Our 1966 production at the Borough Hall was combined with **Trial by Jury**, with *Geoffrey Ford* directing and *William Llewellyn* as musical director.

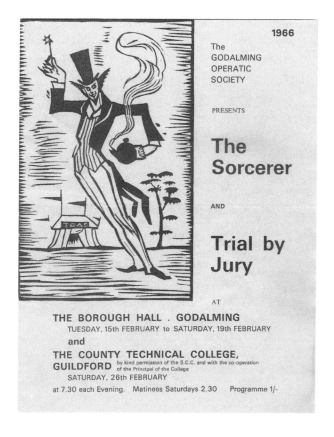

1966

The GODALMING OPERATIC SOCIETY

PRESENTS

The Sorcerer

AND

Trial by Jury

AT

THE BOROUGH HALL . GODALMING
TUESDAY, 15th FEBRUARY to SATURDAY, 19th FEBRUARY
and
THE COUNTY TECHNICAL COLLEGE, GUILDFORD by kind permission of the S.C.C. and with the co-operation of the Principal of the College
SATURDAY, 26th FEBRUARY
at 7.30 each Evening. Matinees Saturdays 2.30 Programme 1/-

THE SORCERER 1966

Meston Reid played the part of Alexis in our 1984 production. *Michael Harding* directed with *Robin Wells* as musical director. *Michael Harding* and *Robin Wells* also directed the 1994 production. Our 2006 production was directed by *Mark Woolgar* with *Robin Wells* as musical director.

THE SORCERER 1984

"THE SPRITES" 1984

Although just three "Sprites" from the 1984 production are featured in the photograph, in the programme there are in fact six names listed. They are:
Rebecca Harding,
Victoria Hartnall,
Sarah Heneage,
Sarah Newholme,
Alison Wells and
Rebecca Wells.

UTOPIA LIMITED

Utopia Limited, or **The Flowers of Progress**, opened on 7th October 1893 at the Savoy Theatre and ran for 245 performances. It was the penultimate collaboration between Gilbert and Sullivan, opening more than two years after **The Gondoliers** had closed. A legal dispute, between Gilbert on the one hand and Carte and Sullivan on the other, became known as the famous "Carpet Quarrel". Despite their subsequent attempts to patch up their relationship, Gilbert, Carte and Sullivan would never again be on the same terms as they had been during the 1880s.

Utopia Limited is the most extravagantly costumed and staged of all the Savoy Operas. It also requires a very large cast. Gilbert's libretto is less tightly constructed than its predecessors and the score represents the nadir of Sullivan's creative output. This may explain why it is revived less often than the earlier operas. But the piece is not without its admirers. George Bernard Shaw stated "I enjoyed the score of **Utopia** more than that of any of the previous Savoy operas".

Utopia Limited also has extra significance for the Society. In 2007 we were invited to take the production to the Waterford International Festival of Light Opera in Ireland (now known as the Waterford International Music Festival). It was quite a challenge to get everything and everybody in place for this one show in Waterford's historic Theatre Royal. Our performance was well received and we had the honour of winning the Adjudicator's Special Award. The production was directed by *Pat O'Connell* with musical direction by *Robin Wells*. Our only other production of **Utopia Limited** was in 1977 when *Desmond Holt* was the producer and *Robin Wells* the musical director.

UTOPIA LIMITED 1977

Utopia Limited is very rarely performed but we were pleased to mount productions in 1977 and 2007, despite the complexity of assembling a large cast.

2007 DRAMATIS PERSONÆ
"UTOPIA LIMITED"

King Paramount	Richard Arthur
Scaphio	Simon Cakebread
Phantis	Lee Power
Tarara	Hammy Sparks
Calynx	Karl King
Captain Fitzbattleaxe	Richard Hales
Lord Dramaleigh	Peter Lucas
Captain Corcoran	Richard Bacon
Mr. Goldbury	Mark Waters
Sir Bailey Barre	Anthony Koller
Mr. Blushington	Tony Budd
The Princess Zara	Ruth Sanders
The Princess Nekaya	Rebecca Lucas
The Princess Kalyba	Sue Starbuck
The Lady Sophie	Nora Price
Phylla	Jessie Howard
Melene	Clare Cunningham
Salata	Alison Reeve
Princess Zara's Handmaid	Lucy Ashe

Chorus of Utopian Ladies:
Sall Baring, Michelle Bradley, Rosie Clark, Margaret Cox, Chris Howard, Barbara Hubble, Janet Hughes, Sheila Knight, Alex Lawrence, Gillian Lucas, Katie Plummer, Joan Robinson, Sue Tilling.

Chorus of Utopian Gentlemen, Life Guards etc:
Len Cook, Harry Evans, Jeff Holliday, Julian Hubble, David Hughes, Alan Knight, Antony Lucas, Peter Melville, Ken Mills, Nathan Morley, Piers Plummer , Eddie Powlesland, Michael Scanlon.

UTOPIA LIMITED 2007

UTOPIA LIMITED 2007

When we took the production of **Utopia Limited** to the Waterford International Festival for our performance on 24th September 2007 there were some changes to the principal roles. They are as follows:

Scaphio	Ian Henderson
Mr. Goldbury	Geoff Vivian
Melene	Chris Howard
Salata	Barbara Saunders

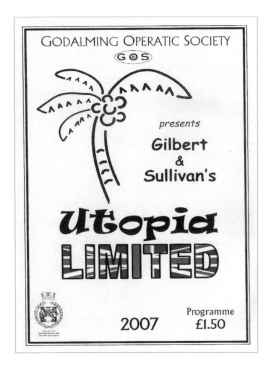

41

The Grand Duke, or **The Statutory Duel**, opened on March 7th 1896 at the Savoy Theatre, London. This, the last G&S opera, ran for only 123 performances. In **The Grand Duke** Gilbert and Sullivan come full circle, back to the theme of their first collaboration: a troupe of actors taking political power. The Grand Duke suffers from many of the same problems as **Utopia Limited** – it has a long and rambling libretto – and it calls for more principal quality voices than the typical G&S opera. Nevertheless, the story contains a number of hilarious moments and funny characters, the settings are colourful and the music is appealingly bright. Some people find this opera to be the most underrated of the G&S works.

A "full circle" was almost completed by the Society with our production of **The Grand Duke** in 2001, directed by *Michael Harding* and *Robin Wells*. **The Grand Duke**, like **Utopia Limited**, is very rarely performed being the only one of the full G&S operas not having previously been performed by us.

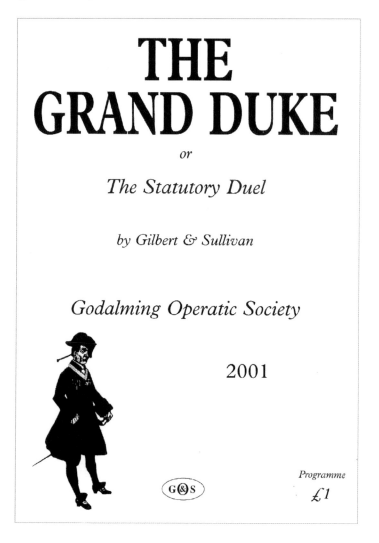

THE GRAND DUKE

or

The Statutory Duel

by Gilbert & Sullivan

Godalming Operatic Society

2001

G&S

Programme

£1

2001 DRAMATIS PERSONÆ
"THE GRAND DUKE"

Rudolph	Mark Waters
Ernest Dumkopf	Geoff Vivian
Ludwig	David Billett
Dr Tannhauser	Laurence Welch
The Prince of Monte Carlo	Hammy Sparks
Ben Hashbaz	Harry Evans
Herald	Peter Gibbs
The Princess of Monte Carlo	Carol Sarson
The Baroness von Krakenfeldt	Sue Starbuck
Julia Jellicoe	Ruth Sanders
Lisa	Diana Harding
Olga	Catharine Humphrys
Gretchen	Rebecca Lucas
Bertha	Sall Baring
Elsa	Emma Dear

Ladies of the Chorus:
Rosa Atkinson, Sue Billett, Kath Brett, Janet Cooper-Tydeman, Margaret Cox, Jane Currie, Anne Gray, Barbara Hubble, Gillian Lucas, Sarah Priston, Jill Payne, Barbara Saunders, Linda Scanlon, Sue Tilling.
Gentlemen of the Chorus:
Ambrose Barber, Tony Budd, Jeff Holliday, Julian Hubble, Peter Lucas, Ken Mills, Michael Scanlon, John Wood.
Dancers:
Terry Butcher, Ruth Auty, Charlotte Boughton.

THE GRAND DUKE 2001

THE GRAND DUKE 2001

As you will see in the preceding section **The Grand Duke** almost completed the "full circle" when we performed it in 2001. In recent years more interest has been shown in Gilbert and Sullivan's first collaboration: **Thespis**. The Society has yet to add this lesser known opera to its list of those performed.

THESPIS

Thespis Act II
From *The Graphic* Feb 1872

Thespis or **The Gods Grown Old** – the first collaboration by Gilbert and Sullivan – was conceived as a Christmas entertainment for John Hollingshead's Gaiety Theatre where it received its first performance on 26ᵗʰ December 1871 and ran for 63 performances. Although it has often been described as a failure, it outlasted most of the Christmas entertainments that season.

Unfortunately, most of the original music for this opera has been lost. Performances today either adapt music from other Sullivan scores, or use a replacement score written by one of several composers.

44

TRIAL BY JURY

The Society has performed **Trial by Jury** as a companion piece on six occasions – the first being in 1939 when our main production was **H.M.S. Pinafore**. You will find the other occasions included in the following chapter.

TRIAL BY JURY 1939
"12 GOOD MEN AND TRUE"

Four years passed after Gilbert and Sullivan had created the 1871 Christmas entertainment **Thespis**. Each became even more eminent in his field, but they did not have occasion to work together. Richard D'Oyly Carte, who was then acting for Selina Dolaro and her company in a season of light opera at the Royalty Theatre, asked the two men to collaborate on a short opera to be played as an after piece to Offenbach's comic opera, *La Périchole*. On 25th March 1875 **Trial by Jury** opened at the Royalty Theatre. The very witty, tuneful and "English" piece was an immediate hit with Londoners and continued to be played until the Royalty closed on 12th June for the summer. **Trial by Jury** was again on the bill when the theatre re-opened on 11th October 1875. The conclusion of Dolaro's season on 18th December 1875 marked the official end of **Trial by Jury's** opening run, by which time it had been performed 131 times.

But clearly **Trial by Jury** continued to find favour with the theatre-going public. From 13th January until 5th May 1876, **Trial by Jury** was on the bill at the Opéra Comique[1] (under the management of Charles Morton) for a run of 96 performances and again from 3rd March to 26th May 1877 at the Royal Strand Theatre, bringing the total number of performances in its first two years to nearly 300.

Trial by Jury is quite short, lasting only forty minutes, and is the only one of the operas to contain no spoken dialogue. Many people consider it to be the most perfectly constructed of the whole series and it is indeed a little gem of wit, sentiment and charm. The absurdities that can come from a breach of promise case, when the sensibilities of the jury and the judge are affected, was just the sort of subject to inspire Gilbert; and the libretto he produced in turn inspired Sullivan to write some of his most sparkling music.

The part of the judge in the first production was played by Fred Sullivan, the composer's brother.

1. Although advertised as opening on the 13th, it was not actually performed that evening owing to the other items on the programme overrunning

CHAPTER 5
OTHER PRODUCTIONS
AND SUMMER CONCERTS

In Chapter 4: "The Operas" you may have noticed that on occasions an additional one-act operetta was included on the same bill as a "curtain–raiser" companion piece to some of the shorter main operas such as **The Pirates of Penzance**. We now tend to perform just one of the main operas; but we also enjoy the opportunity to perform the shorter one-act ones too. Some of these one-act operettas have also been performed as part of our Summer Concert.

We first performed **Cox and Box**, or **The Long-Lost Brothers**, in 1936. The libretto was written by Sir Francis Cowley Burnand, who was also a great contributor to Punch, and the music was by Sir Arthur Sullivan. Sullivan wrote this piece in 1866 – five years before his first opera with Gilbert. In its day **Cox and Box** was an extremely popular one-act opera. We confess that our 1936 programme incorrectly describes **Cox and Box** as being by Gilbert and Sullivan. We also performed **Cox and Box** in 1990 as a companion piece. In 2006 we performed it at Churt Village Hall and again as part of a concert at the Electric Theatre in Guildford in 2010.

COX AND BOX 1990

Trial by Jury, like **Cox and Box**, has been more frequently performed as a companion piece to one of the main operas. Although it is a one-act opera it is, nevertheless, very compelling and amusing. Our first performance was as the companion to **H.M.S. Pinafore** in 1939. We performed it again as a companion piece in 1955, 1966, 1978, 1988 and 1997. In 2004 we performed it as part of our Summer Concert. There is more information about **Trial by Jury** in the Chapter 4 "The Operas 1925 to 2012".

TRIAL BY JURY 1988

The **Zoo**, by Bolton Rowe and Arthur Sullivan was our companion piece to **The Pirates of Penzance** in 1981.

THE ZOO 1981

For World Refugee Year on 25th May 1960, Owen Brannigan, a renowned opera singer, gave a concert at the Borough Hall on behalf of the Godalming Branch of the United Nations Society. He was accompanied by *William Llewellyn* and members of the Society. The musical director on that occasion was *David Stone.*

When the Godalming Music Festival was first established it took place in the month of May. This month was chosen deliberately to avoid clashing with our annual G&S production. During the late 1960s, however, Festival events moved to March and so it was no longer viable for the Society to formally participate in the competitions. The Society then gave other performances at various times, including the introduction of the Summer Concerts. Details of our other performances are listed at the end of this chapter.

In April 1975 we presented **Gilbert and Sullivan for All** at the Civic Hall in Guildford. Ian Kennedy was the musical director on this occasion. For many years Ian had a great interest in Sullivan's music. In 1974 he joined the **Gilbert and Sullivan for All** tours to America, Australia, New Zealand and the Far East.

Gilbert and Sullivan for All performed in April, 1981 and again at the Civic Hall in Guildford, starring *Donald Adams* and *Thomas Round.* Both gentlemen had played principal roles with D'Oyly Carte.

Also in 1981 Godalming celebrated its centenary of being the first town in the world to have a public electricity supply. Coincidentally, it was also the centenary year of the Savoy Theatre being the first in the world to be illuminated by electric light. At the time, in 1881, **Patience** was being performed at the Savoy. We contributed to Godalming's centenary celebration by performing a concert version of **Patience.**

It would be less than honest if we did not admit that, at times, things did not always go to plan. I recall two such events in 2010. The first was **Celebrating Surrey** at Loseley Park on 26th June. We were invited to perform on one of the stages but on arrival we found that no piano was available. After some frantic searching, a Clavinova was produced. We then performed several numbers from **The Yeomen of the Guard**, despite a large number of drummers processing in the vicinity and a certain amount of bell ringing!

The second event was participating in **Celebrating the Theatre** in Guildford on 30th June 2010. At The Electric Theatre we planned to perform the one-act operetta **Cox and Box** as the second part of a concert. However, a few days before the concert, we discovered the other organisation had withdrawn. We were asked if we could perform a full show, including **Cox and Box**, which we did successfully. The whole evening was wonderfully entertaining but due to circumstances beyond our control, there was only a very small audience. Nevertheless we displayed excellent stoicism. To paraphrase a well known statement: "That never in the field of entertainment has so much been given by so many for so few".

As you may have noticed in Chapter 1 "Setting the Scene", the Society is not all about G&S. We have, from time to time, performed at many local venues. We are also invited to give smaller group performances at various special events. These extra performances mean that we have the opportunity not only to entertain but also to promote the Society as a whole. By doing so, we aim to reach a wider audience, by encouraging people to come to enjoy our annual Gilbert and Sullivan production. One such special event in 1974 was our performance of an abridged concert version of **The Mikado** in Guildford Cathedral.

In recent years our Summer Concerts have been performed at The Electric Theatre, Guildford. These Summer Concerts tend to be light–hearted and informal; we have, on a number of occasions, selected a topic or a theme to form the core of the concert. At times the whole concert follows the core theme throughout but on other occasions a one-act opera has been included.

The Summer Concerts began in 1971 because we needed to fill the gap that had been created when the dates of the Godalming Music Festival were changed to earlier in the year. In later years the Summer Concerts, as we now know them today, were born out of the idea of a soirée. At the time Clandon House was an ideal intimate venue. *Michael Hartnall*, *Robin Wells* and *Betty Moat* were very much involved in the planning of this new venture. The new format proved to be successful and we have continued to use it – albeit in the slightly larger Electric Theatre.

Our concerts also give those members, who have not had a major part in the annual G&S production, the opportunity to perform solos, or duets, in addition to the chorus items.

The one-act operas performed at the Summer Concerts have included **The Batsman's Bride** – words by Donald Hughes and music by Percy Heywood and **Perseverance** – words by A.P.Herbert and music by Vivian Ellis.

In 2008 our Summer Concert took place at Godalming Borough Hall. On this occasion we performed the one-act operetta **A Frank Affair**, which was written especially for the Society by Eric Thompson and, Society member, *Ambrose Barber*. The music was by our musical director *Robin Wells* and *Sir Arthur Sullivan* in equal measure.

Listed below are many of our other productions and Summer Concerts. You will also find listed Musical Directors (MD:) Producers (P:), Accompanists (A:) and other notes.

DATE & VENUE	TITLE	MUSICAL DIRECTORS PRODUCERS ACCOMPANISTS AND OTHER NOTES.
25.5.60 Borough Hall Godalming	**A Concert on behalf of Godalming U.N. Society**	With Owen Brannigan A: William Llewellyn MD: David Stone
23 3.68 Charterhouse Chapel	**Verdi Requiem (A joint concert with Charterhouse)**	Performed with other choirs MD: William Llewellyn. Orchestra Leader Geoffrey Ford
25.5.68 Godalming Library	**Centenary Concert for Congregational Church**	MD: David Stone A: William Llewellyn
12.6.71 Shalford Village Hall	**An Evening with Godalming Operatic Society**	MD: Robin Wells With Jennifer Monk, Ellen Rowell and Eileen Skelton In aid of W. Surrey Cheshire Home
30.9.72 Charterhouse	**Musical Evening G&S excerpts**	MD: William Llewellyn
Oct 72 Charterhouse	**The Pilgrims Progress**	MD: William Llewellyn A joint production with Charterhouse
12.5.73 Borough Hall, Godalming	**An Evening with GOS**	MD: Robin Wells Orchestra Leader Ralph Truckle
24.4.74 Guildford Cathedral	**Your Music Night**	Organ: Caleb Fawcett. Plus Guildford Light Orchestra and Westborough Singers
19.4.75 Guildford Civic Hall	**Gilbert and Sullivan for All**	MD: Ian Kennedy

10.12.75 Aldershot	**A Christmas Concert**	With the Staff Band of the RAMC
29.5.76 Guildford Civic Hall	**An Evening of Gilbert and Sullivan**	Presented by Ian Wallace MD: Robin Wells Orchestra Leader Sally Brundan
26.4.78 St. Saviour's Hall, Guildford	**An Evening of G & S**	A: Ellen Brown
20.5.78 Guildford Civic Hall	**Verdi's Aida (concert version)**	MD: Robin Wells Orchestra Leader Sally Brundan
28.4.79 Charterhouse Hall	**An Evening with Gilbert and Sullivan**	Introduced by William Llewellyn MD: Robin Wells
15.9.79 Rudgwick Village Hall	**Gilbert and Sullivan**	MD: Robin Wells A: Ellen Brown
7.6.80 Borough Hall, Godalming	**Merrie England (concert version)**	MD: Robin Wells Orchestra Leader Sally Brundan
14.6.80 Godalming United Church	**GOS In Concert**	A: Ellen Brown
25.4.81 Guilford Civic Hall	**Gilbert and Sullivan for All**	Starring Donald Adams and Thomas Round
19.9.81 Borough Hall, Godalming	**Patience (Concert version). Celebrating the centenary of Godalming's public electricity supply**	MD: William Llewellyn
21.5.82 St Catherine's School, Bramley	**A Concert including some G&S**	
7.5.83 Clandon House	**Upstairs-Downstairs**	MD: Robin Wells A: Ellen Brown P: Michael Harding
9.6.84 Clandon House	**Month in – Month out**	MD: Robin Wells A: Robin Wells and Ellen Brown P: Betty Moat
12.12.84 Onslow Village Hall	**Christmas Entertainment**	A: Ellen Brown
18.6.85 Clandon House	**Two by Two**	MD: Ellen Brown A: Robin Wells P: Betty Moat
18.5.86 Borough Hall, Godalming	**A Concert with Richard Baker**	MD: William Llewellyn With Charterhouse Choir & Symphony Orchestra
7.6.86 Clandon House	**Sing a Song of Europe**	MD: Robin Wells A: Margaret Patience P: Betty Moat
30.5.87 Clandon House	**On Sea & Shore, or I do Like to be Beside the Seaside**	MD: Robin Wells A: Margaret Patience P: Betty Moat
12.12.87 Elstead	**An Entertainment**	
4.6.88 Clandon House	**Distant Lands**	MD: Robin Wells A: Margaret Patience P: Betty Moat
11.6.88 Rake Court, Milford	**An Evening of Music with GOS**	MD/A: Robin Wells P: Betty Moat

17.12.88 Borough Hall, Godalming	**An Evening of Music and Song**	MD: Robin Wells With Godalming Town Band. Director of Music David Wright
3.6.89 Clandon House	**The Heavens are Telling**	A: Robin Wells P: Betty Moat. Guest Artist Meston Reid
2.11.89 Cranleigh Arts Centre	**Godalming Operatic Entertains**	Accompanist Margaret Patience
9.6.90 Clandon House	**A Feast of Music or Food, Glorious Food**	MD: Robin Wells A: Margaret Patience P: Betty Moat
22.6.91 Clandon House	**The Music of Monarchs**	MD: Robin Wells A: Margaret Patience P: Betty Moat
14.4.92 Cranleigh Village Hall	**GOS Concert**	P: Betty Moat
5.6.92 Guildford Civic Hall	**Music for a Friday Night. Celebrating the Lives of G&S With Richard Baker**	MD: Robin Wells MD: for Richard Baker· Patrick Healy
14.5.93 Guildford Civic Hall	**GOS & Richard Baker "Request the Pleasure"**	MDs: Robin Wells and Patrick Healy
9.10.93 Borough Hall, Godalming	**Light Fantastic**	A concert for "Go Godalming" Christmas Lights Appeal
3.7.94 Tithe Barn, Loseley Park	**Mirror of Great Britain**	MD: Robin Wells A: Jean Tombs P: Betty Moat
6.5.95 Borough Hall, Godalming	**Gala Concert celebrating 50th anniversary of V.E. Day**	MD: Robin Wells Orchestra Leader Sally Dewey
14.6.97 The Electric Theatre	**Hiawatha's Wedding Feast and The Batsman's Bride**	MD: Robin Wells A: Brenda Stokes P: Michael Harding Commentator: David Rayvern-Allen
20.6.98 Ben Travers Theatre, Charterhouse	**Lucifer's Lyrics**	MD: Robin Wells A: Edward Moulding P: Betty Moat
29.5.99 The Electric Theatre	**Moving to the Millennium or Music of the 20th Century**	MD: Robin Wells A: Edward Moulding Stage Direction and Choreography: Anne Gray
8.7.2000 The Electric Theatre	**Musical Magic**	MD: Robin Wells A: Edward Moulding Stage Direction and Choreography: Anne Gray
9.6.01 Borough Hall, Godalming and on 16.6.01 The Electric Theatre	**Oh What a Lovely War**	MD: Robin Wells A: A small orchestra P: Veronica Marchbanks Choreography: Anne Gray
22.6.02 The Electric Theatre	**Two by Two**	MD: Robin Wells A: Helen Dives P: Hammy Sparks
11.1.03 Cranleigh Village Hall	**Concert for Cranleigh Arts and Crafts Club**	Accompanist Helen Dives
14.6.03 The Electric Theatre	**Food Glorious Food and Cox and Box**	MD: Robin Wells A: Helen Dives P: Hammy Sparks P: For Cox and Box David Dray

14.5.04 Guildford Masonic Centre	**Concert for the "Ladies Club"**	A: Jean Tombs
6.6.04 The Electric Theatre	**Law & Disorder and Trial by Jury**	MD Robin Wells P: Hammy Sparks
12.10.04 Charterhouse Music School	**I Have a Song to Sing-O!**	MD/A: Robin Wells
29.5.05 The Electric Theatre	**Rags to Riches and Perseverance**	MD/A: Robin Wells P: Hammy Sparks
21.10.05 Priorsfield School	**The Mayor of Godalming's Trafalgar Dinner**	MD: Robin Wells For the bi-centenary of the Battle of Trafalgar
5.5.06 Guildford Masonic Centre	**G&S and other pieces**	MD/A: Robin Wells
27.5.06 Parish Church Ss Peter & Paul	**Wedding of John and Penny Graham's daughter**	A: Robin Wells
3.6.06 The Electric Theatre	**Bridegroom & Bride and The Batsman's Bride**	MD/A: Robin Wells P: Hammy Sparks
2.12.06 Churt Village Hall	**Cox & Box as part of a Supper Evening in aid of St. Johns Church, Churt**	MD/A: Robin Wells P: David Dray
13.1 07 Cranleigh Village Hall	**Programme for Cranleigh Arts**	MD: Robin Wells
3.6.07 The Electric Theatre	**A Transport of Delight**	MD/A: Robin Wells P: Hammy Sparks and Irene Wright
7.6.08 Borough Hall, Godalming and on 14.6.08 Churt Village Hall	**Sing a Song of Sixpence and A Frank Affair**	MD/A: Robin Wells P: Hammy Sparks Choreographer: Irene Wright
17.9.08 Guildhall, Guildford	**Surrey Hills Society Launch Party**	A: Nick Morrice
20.1.09 Godalming Museum	**Concert for the opening of the "I Have a Song to Sing-O" Exhibition**	A: Robin Wells
13.6.09 The Electric Theatre	**The Circle of Life**	MD/A: Robin Wells P: Irene Wright
25.7.09 Guildford Country Club	**Surrey Hills Society Dinner**	A: Barbara Jackson
22.5.10 The Electric Theatre	**Let's Talk about the Weather**	MD/A: Robin Wells P: Irene Wright
5.6.10 Woking Festival of Volunteering	**Some numbers from our Summer Concert**	A: Robin Wells
26.6.10 Loseley Park	**Celebrating Surrey**	MD/A: Robin Wells.
30.6.10 The Electric Theatre	**A Concert including Cox and Box**	MD/A: Robin Wells.
3.10.10 The Tithe Barn, Loseley Park	**A Special Concert to celebrate Brian & Pat Oxborough's Ruby Wedding celebrations**	A: Robin Wells
8.1.11 Cranleigh Village Hall	**A Concert for Cranleigh Arts & Crafts Society**	A: Robin Wells.
11.6.11 The Electric Theatre	**Oh! to be in England**	MD/A: Robin Wells P: Irene Wright

CHAPTER 6
MUSICAL DIRECTORS

The Society has been extremely fortunate in that in all the years since it was formed, it has had only six musical directors – all of whom, barring our first one, have been music masters from Charterhouse. Those from Charterhouse have had a strong association with the Godalming Music Festival since it began in 1947. Ralph Vaughan Williams was a strong supporter of the Festival and he also presented the certificates.

Dr A.A. Mackintosh D.Mus. B.Mus. FRCO
Dr A.A. Mackintosh was the first musical director in 1925. He was organist and choirmaster at Godalming Parish Church. Dr Mackintosh held the position at the church from 1891 to 1936; but unfortunately, he had to resign after our first production due to ill health.

Arthur Trew Hon ARCM
Arthur Trew was our musical director from 1926 to 1957 and the first who came from Charterhouse. He was also a well-known cellist. Apart from his long association with the Society, Mr Trew was very much involved in the establishment of the Godalming Music Festival when it began in 1947. Family involvement featured on many occasions, as Mr Trew's wife was a percussionist in the orchestra. In his childhood, Mr Trew attended productions that were personally directed by W.S. Gilbert. Mr Trew was not without a sense of humour: when rehearsing **The Gondoliers** he would, with a twinkle in his eye, remind people to sing "wine in abundance", not "a bun dance"!

David Stone B.Mus. FRAM FRSAMD
David Stone was musical director from 1958 to 1962. He too was a master at Charterhouse from 1947. He also played 1st violin in our orchestra. In 1956 Mr Stone joined the BBC Music Division and was Senior Producer of Chamber Music and Recitals. From 1969 to 1981 he was the Director of the School of Music at the Royal Scottish Academy of Music and Drama. Like Arthur Trew before him, Mr Stone maintained a strong association with the Godalming Music Festival. He is currently an Honorary President of the Festival.

William Llewellyn MBE B.Mus. FRAM ARCO

William Llewellyn succeeded David Stone as musical director in 1963 and remained until 1968. He too was a master at Charterhouse before becoming Director of Music there. Like his Charterhouse predecessors, Mr Llewellyn's contribution to the Society, other organisations and the Godalming Music Festival cannot be underestimated. Apart from his role of Musical Director for the Society, Mr Llewellyn was a Festival adjudicator in 1962, a committee member from 1963 and Chairman from 1968 to 1984. Mr Llewellyn, who was our President from 1970 to 1991, is a Life Member of the Society.

George Draper

George Draper was our Musical Director for the 1969 and 1970 productions. Mr Draper – an ex-Guardsman – was a brilliant clarinettist and Head of Wind and Brass at Charterhouse. Remarkably he was able to play every wind and brass instrument as well as the violin! While he was at Charterhouse there was an occasion when a piper was needed for an event being held there. Mr Draper duly obliged by learning the bagpipes! He was also soloist at the Children's Day Concert in 1949 when the certificates were presented by Vaughan Williams. As well as playing clarinet in our orchestra from 1947, Mr Draper also maintained strong links with the Godalming Music Festival.

Robin Wells FRCO GRSM ARCM Hon ARAM

Born in Suffolk, Robin, our current Musical Director and Vice-President of the Society, studied for four years at The Royal College of Music during which period he became a graduate of the Royal Schools of Music and a Fellow of the Royal College of Organists. In 1965 Robin joined the staff of Charterhouse as an assistant music master. In September 1987 he succeeded William Llewellyn as Director of Music. He retired from Charterhouse in 2003.

For many years Robin has been an examiner for The Associated Board of the Royal Schools of Music which has taken him all over the United Kingdom, as well as to the Far East and to New Zealand. Locally, he is also the conductor of the Farnham & Bourne Choral Society.

Robin was Chairman of Godalming Music Festival for 19 years and Director of the Charterhouse Summer School of Music for 24 years. From 1995 to 2000 he was conductor of the Petersfield Musical Festival. As a further tribute, to his excellent achievements, Robin is now an Honorary Associate of the Royal Academy of Music.

Robin's first association with Godalming Operatic Society was in 1966 when he acted as chorus master for the 1967 production of **Iolanthe**. In 1970 he succeeded George Draper as the Society's Musical Director for the 1971 production of **Princess Ida**. Robin is also an Honorary President of the Godalming Music Festival. In 2010 Robin celebrated his 40th year as our musical director. You will find more information in Chapter 4 "The Operas".

CHAPTER 7
PRODUCERS

In our early years the tendency was to refer to those who directed as the Producer. In recent years, the term Stage Director has become more common. However, in Chapter 4: "The Operas", I have generally used the term Producer.

In the time since the Society was formed in 1925, we have had only 20 producers. No less than 11 of our producers had performed principal roles for D'Oyly Carte.

In the Chapter 8: "The D'Oyly Carte Opera Company", you will find background information relating to those 11 producers, together with some notes in respect of their performances with the company.

Irrespective of the D'Oyly Carte connection, we have enjoyed the services of many fine producers. It is equally important to portray their contribution to the Society's many successful years.

Producer for **The Yeomen of the Guard** in 1925 was *Herbert Shindler*. He also produced the **The Pirates of Penzance** and played the part of the Major General in 1928.

Geoffrey Ford was our producer from 1965 to 1968. During that time he directed **Ruddigore, The Sorcerer, Trial by Jury, Iolanthe** and **H.M.S. Pinafore**. From 1957 to 1992 Mr Ford, who was Head of Strings at Charterhouse, played violin in the orchestra. He also had a strong association with the Godalming Music Festival.

Desmond Holt produced our first production of **Utopia Limited** in 1977. Mr Holt also directed productions for Godalming Theatre Group, which he founded in 1964. In 2001 a Memorial Trust was created in his name. *Keith Thomas*, also from GTG, was choreographer for the 1977 production.

Michael Harding had a long and illustrious career. Starting in 1962 and spanning some 40 years with the Society, Michael was both a performer and in various years a producer. Additionally he was our Business Manager in the 1970s. His first show as producer was **H.M.S. Pinafore** in 1978, culminating with **The Gondoliers** in 2002. Michael's wife, *Diana*, also played principal roles on various occasions. In 1983 Michael produced our first Summer Concert at Clandon House and in 1997 he produced our first Summer Concert at the Electric Theatre. A special cake was made by Diana for our Golden Jubilee celebrations in 1975. Michael died on 6th November 2002.

Doris Relph trained as a singer at the Guildhall School of Music. Following a career in opera she produced a number of the major classical operas of Mozart, Puccini and Verdi. In 1975 she produced "Oliver" in Jamaica and in 1977 went to Nassau in the Bahamas to produce "Let's Make an Opera" by Benjamin Britten. Miss Relph produced **Princess Ida** for the Society in 1982.

Carole Mudie came from a musical family. Her mother, Elizabeth Aveling, sang opposite Richard Tauber and her father, Michael Mudie, was musical director at Sadler's Wells. Carole's grandfather, Claude Aveling, met Sir Arthur Sullivan when he was Registrar at the Royal College of Music. Sullivan passed on to him the correct speeds of many of the numbers in the Savoy Operas and in turn these were passed on to Sir Malcolm Sargent when he conducted the operas in 1929.

Carole played several of the leading soprano roles in the Savoy Operas before she trained at the Royal Academy of Music. She then gained further experience in West End musicals, opera and cabaret. Before producing **Iolanthe** for us in 1995 she had directed "No No Nanette", "Oklahoma!", "The 1940s Show" and music hall.

Hammy Sparks joined the Society in 1975. He became the Society's Chairman in 2003 until 2012 when he stood down at the Annual General Meeting. At the 2012 AGM *Michael Hartnall* paid tribute to Hammy for his outstanding contribution, both as Chairman and as a performer. Hammy has continued to perform annually with the Society, mostly in principal roles, since 1976 – the only exception was in 2003 when he produced **Princess Ida**.

Hammy taught mathematics at Charterhouse for 37 years. For three years he was Director of the Ben Travers Theatre at Charterhouse. His productions included Breaker Morant, Hail Caesar! and Equus. Our Summer Concerts from 2002 to 2008 were also produced by him. Apart from his interest in all forms of theatre Hammy's other interests include paddle steamers and narrow gauge railways. Hammy is a Life Member of the Society.

Mark Woolgar was our producer for three years. His first production was **The Mikado** in 2004, when we moved from the Civic Hall in Guildford to the Leatherhead Theatre. This was followed by **Iolanthe** in 2005, which we also performed at The International Gilbert and Sullivan Festival in Buxton, and **The Sorcerer** in 2006. Over 40 years previously, Mark had directed **Iolanthe** at the Oxford Playhouse while he was a schoolmaster. Mark subsequently joined the theatrical profession via trainee directorship with the Bristol Old Vic Company where he stayed for four years. After nearly 200 productions he then became Director of Derby Playhouse for seven years. In addition, Mark has toured widely with his own Oscar Wilde show.

Pat O'Connell's first production for the Society was **Utopia Limited** in 2007. We also took the production to The Waterford International Festival of Light Opera in September 2007. Pat has produced all our productions since 2007 – the most recent being **The Pirates of Penzance** in 2012. He has been a member of various operatic societies since childhood. Pat has an impressive tally in the region of 150 shows in 46 years as an actor, singer, dancer, impresario and producer and, for the last 17 years, as a director.

The Society was delighted and honoured to receive an invitation to perform the 2012 production of **The Pirates of Penzance** – under Pat's direction – at the 19th International Gilbert and Sullivan Festival in the magnificent Opera House in Buxton, to much acclaim.

CHAPTER 8
THE D'OYLY CARTE OPERA COMPANY

"By kind permission of R. D'Oyly Carte Esq"

or

"By kind permission of Bridget D'Oyly Carte"

The above statement appeared in all our programmes until 1961. After 1961 copyright on Gilbert's words had expired and permission for the Society to perform the G&S operas was no longer needed. The 'R. D'Oyly Carte' referred to above is Richard D'Oyly Carte's son Rupert. Bridget succeeded Rupert following his death in 1948.

When licensing amateur companies to perform the G&S operas, strict rules were laid down by Rupert D'Oyly Carte. Approved productions were required to closely follow the libretto, score and the D'Oyly Carte production staging. Rupert expected the highest possible standard of production with special attention to clear enunciation. These high standards were also required when Bridget D'Oyly Carte inherited Rupert's role.

It is worth mentioning here that one of the strongest characteristics of the Society today is that we maintain the highest standard in the tradition of D'Oyly Carte.

After the last copyright of the G&S operas had expired in 1961 Bridget D'Oyly Carte set up and endowed a charitable trust that presented the operas. Unfortunately, mounting costs and a lack of public funding forced the closure of the company in 1982. Although a new company was formed in 1988 it did not perform continuously, owing to the lack of significant funding. It suspended productions in 2003.

As will be seen in Chapter 4: "The Operas", much reference has been made to many of our Producers who had performed with the D'Oyly Carte Company. Over the years between 1926 and 1996, we have had no less than 11 producers who had performed with the Company – most of whom played principal roles. Short profiles of their D'Oyly Carte careers are listed below.

Two other former D'Oyly Carte principals performed at our special concert **Gilbert and Sullivan for All**, in 1981. I have also included information about them in the short profiles.

Hugh Enes Blackmore

Hugh Enes Blackmore joined us as producer in 1926 to direct **Princess Ida**. He was joined by his wife, Tessa (née Snelson) to direct **The Gondoliers** in 1927. They then directed all our productions, except for 1928, right up until 1939.

The career of Hugh Enes Blackmore (or Blackie as he was known to his friends and colleagues) began in 1893. He was also referred to as the "Iron Throated Tenor"! Mr Blackmore also had the distinction of performing under the direction of W.S. Gilbert, who introduced him to his wife to be, Tessa, on stage at the Savoy Theatre. Mr Blackmore's first role in 1893 was that of Sir Bailey-Barre in **Utopia Limited** at the Savoy until the show closed in June 1894. He also toured with D'Oyly Carte until he left the Company in 1896. In 1908

Mr Blackmore rejoined D'Oyly Carte and played various roles until he finally left the Company in 1919.

Tessa Snelson

Tessa Snelson was married to Hugh Enes Blackmore (see previous section).

Tessa was with the Company for three separate periods: 1892 to 1895, 1908 to 1909 and from 1915 to 1923. Tessa started in the chorus in 1892. She also toured in 1894 until she left in 1895. In 1908 Tessa returned to the Savoy to sing in the chorus. She toured again and played some principal roles until 1909. In 1915 Tessa returned to the D'Oyly Carte Repertory Opera Company to sing in the chorus until 1923 (although for a short period in 1922 she was with the D'Oyly Carte "New" Opera Company). Tessa and her husband Hugh were charter members of the Gilbert & Sullivan Society in London. Tessa died in September 1939.

Clara Dow

For our first production after the Second World War in 1947 we engaged the services of Clara Dow to produce **The Gondoliers.** Miss Dow also produced our shows in 1948 and 1950. In the section about **The Gondoliers**, in Chapter 4, Miss Dow is described in our programme as "Late Prima Donna The D'Oyly Carte Opera Company".

Miss Dow was another performer who had the distinction of being directed by W.S. Gilbert. She is remembered as one of the last principal sopranos personally trained by W.S. Gilbert at the Savoy. Before joining the Company she studied at the Royal College of Music and did extensive oratorio and concert work. Miss Dow joined the Company in 1906 to sing in the chorus. In 1907 she started to perform principal roles, either at the Savoy or on tour, until 1909 when she left the Company. Miss Dow returned for a short time in 1911 and then again in July 1913 until December 1914.

Leo Sheffield

Leo Sheffield produced **Iolanthe** for us in 1949.

Mr Sheffield was a baritone and also had three separate periods with the Company: 1906 to 1909, 1915 to 1928 and from 1929 to 1930. He too performed at the Savoy and toured with the Company. For many years Mr Sheffield appeared in most of the G&S operas playing a great number of principal roles.

C.William Morgan

In 1951 C William "Billy" Morgan joined us to produce **The Yeomen of the Guard**. With the exception of 1956, he directed all our productions up until 1964.

Mr Morgan was with the D'Oyly Carte organisation for over 30 years: from 1920 to 1950. He performed in the chorus as well as being an understudy and a small-part player. In his later years Mr Morgan performed a number of principal roles. In his last two seasons with the Company he served both on stage and as assistant stage manager. Mr Morgan also performed in **The Yeomen of the Guard** on a great number of occasions.

B.W. Holmes

B.William "Bertie" Holmes was our producer for **The Mikado** in 1956

Mr Holmes was with the Company from 1919 to 1925 and then again from 1940 to 1944. He too was in the chorus originally but he also played some principal roles in his first period with the Company. Mr Holmes returned as a wartime replacement in 1940 to sing again in the chorus. He became the Company's assistant manager in 1943, but continued to sing in the chorus until 1944. Mr Morgan remained with the Company until 1961.

Leonard Osborn

Leonard Osborn joined us in 1969 to produce **The Gondoliers**. He remained with us until 1976.

Mr Osborn had two performing periods with the Company: from 1937 to 1940 and from 1946 to 1959. He too was in the chorus initially, but graduated to principal roles. In 1940 Mr Osborn joined the Royal Air Force. After the war he rejoined the Company to appear in **The Gondoliers**. Although he left the Company in 1959 he returned in 1977 as production director for **Princess Ida**: the special Sadler's Wells Jubilee season. Mr Osborn was also the production director for **Princess Ida** at a Royal Command Performance at Windsor Castle in September 1977.

Cynthia Morey

Cynthia Morey produced **The Yeomen of the Guard** 1980 and **The Pirates of Penzance** in 1981.

Cynthia joined the Company in 1951. Initially she was in the chorus but progressed to playing small parts. In 1954 she was promoted to principal soprano. Cynthia left the company in 1957 to join the Sadler's Wells Opera Company. She appeared in a number of West End musicals and also toured Australia and New Zealand. Cynthia is currently President of the Gilbert & Sullivan Society.

Meston Reid

Meston Reid was our producer for **H.M.S. Pinafore** in 1988 and continued as producer until 1993. He also performed in our 1984 production of **The Sorcerer**, playing the part of Alexis.

Meston was with the Company from 1974 to 1982. He was with Sadler's Wells Opera before joining D'Oyly Carte. He played a number of principal roles and remained with the Company to its final days in February 1982. Meston then sang with the Scottish Chamber Orchestra and toured Scotland on two occasions. Sadly, Meston died at the early age of 48 in October 1993.

James Conroy-Ward

James Conroy-Ward produced our 1996 production of **Ruddigore**.

Mr Conroy-Ward was formally with the Company from 1973 to 1982 although he had, in fact, appeared on stage with them in the 1950's, playing Tom Tucker in **H.M.S. Pinafore** and Ko-Ko's assistant in **The Mikado**. During his later tenure with the Company he played a number of principal roles. Following the closure of the Company Mr Conroy-Ward went into the music publishing business.

Paul Weakley

Paul Weakley performed principal roles with us in 1997, 1998, 1999 and 2002. He also assisted in directing our 2002 production of **The Gondoliers**.

Paul was with the Company for a comparatively short time. He joined the chorus in January 1979 until August 1980. Since leaving the Company Paul has retained a great interest in G&S.

Donald Adams and Thomas Round

On 25th April 1981 we presented a special concert at the Civic Hall, Guildford entitled **Gilbert & Sullivan for All** starring Donald Adams and Thomas Round.

Donald Adams

Donald Adams had a long and illustrious career with the Company from 1951 to 1969 and played a great number of principal parts. He made a number of recordings and appeared in three of the Brent Walker television productions of G & S operas. Mr Adams later performed principal roles with the Welsh National Opera, the English National Opera, Glyndebourne Festival Opera, the Royal Opera and abroad.

Thomas Round

Like Donald Adams, Thomas Round had a distinguished career with the Company over three different periods. In 1969, along with Donald Adams and Norman Meadmore, Mr Round founded the **Gilbert & Sullivan for All** productions.

GODALMING OPERATIC SOCIETY

will present

"GILBERT & SULLIVAN FOR ALL"

starring

DONALD ADAMS and THOMAS ROUND

at the

CIVIC HALL, GUILDFORD.

on

SATURDAY 25th APRIL, 1981 at 7.30 p.m.

Box Office Will Open On 6th April

CHAPTER 9
PERSONALITIES AND PERFORMERS
AND CURRENT LIFE MEMBERS

Since 1925 many people have made valuable contributions to bring the Society to that which it is today. It is clear that over the years – and even today – that a vast amount of teamwork is needed to get the show on the road.

The Society appreciates that many members, as well as performing, do a vast amount of work behind the scenes. For some people membership of the Society has been a family affair too. The surnames of Streeter, Hart, Moat and Brown have been particularly synonymous with the Society over a number of years. It is also true to say, during their membership of the Society, that quite a few members met their future partners.

Many of our members have given exceptionally long service. It is not possible to list every member of the Society and to describe their role; I would need to write a second volume of this book! I hope that the list below gives recognition to those who have made a significant contribution in a variety of roles over the years. Omission from the list does not mean that the value of the work carried out by other members is in any way diminished.

While I was writing this book I discovered that some of my chorus colleagues had been performing in our productions for more than 25 years. Although their appearances have not been entirely continuous over the years, they are included in my list.

Most of the profiles given are quite short but they nevertheless portray the important role that each person has played during the time that they were associated with the Society. You will find two of the profiles are a bit longer than all the others. One is about Fred Jeffrey, who was a performer, and the other is about Ralph Truckle, who was a member of the orchestra. They both lived until their mid-90s. Their stories epitomise what it is to be a part of the "family" of Godalming Operatic Society and its rich heritage.

Miss Daphne F. Barnes
Miss Barnes was a founder member, the Society's first Hon. Secretary and appeared in the 1925 production of **The Yeomen of the Guard**.

Mr G.F. Barrington
Mr Barrington performed a principal role in **The Yeomen of the Guard** in 1925. In later years he was Hon. Secretary and Stage Manager.

Gerald Bartlett
Gerald Bartlett's first performance was in the chorus of **The Pirates of Penzance** in 1959. Gerald was always willing to do anything he could for the Society. During the 1960s Gerald was our Treasurer. He was succeeded in that role by the current President, Michael Hartnall in 1969. Gerald sometimes performed parts – more often than not at the Society's behest than at his own wish! One particularly happy appearance was as Old Adam in the Golden Jubilee production of **Ruddigore**. Gerald was always coming to the Society's rescue with his big car, filling it with all the usual impedimenta and often towing the trailer from A to B. It was through Gerald that a home was found for scenery and props. His last appearance,

before his tragic death, was in **Princess Ida** in 1982. Gerald's wife Barbara (Brignall) was in the chorus in the late 1950s.

C.E. Bateman

Charles Bateman was a member of the Society from 1931 (when he played the Second Yeoman in **The Yeomen of the Guard**). Charles was an excellent tenor and was a member until 1963. His daughter still supports the Society as a Patron.

David and Sue Billett

David Billett's first appearance was in **Utopia Limited** in 1977, when he played the part of Mr Blushington. David played a number of principal roles during his time with the Society. His final appearance was in **Princess Ida** in 2003, when he played the part of Arac. His wife Susan (née Maxwell) featured in the chorus for three separate spells between 1979 and 2003. At times they both served on the committee. Sue was also a very active member of the Social Committee.

Frederick Blizzard

Frederick Blizzard first performed in 1939 in the chorus. He returned to the Society after WW2 until his last appearance in 1954, as a principal in **The Gondoliers**.

Tom Briggs

Tom played a number of principal roles beginning with Richard Dauntless in **Ruddigore** 1986. His last principal role was as Sir Joseph Porter in **H.M.S. Pinafore** in 1997. Tom is the proprietor of Record Corner in Godalming and the shop sells tickets for our annual G&S production.

Ellen Brown (née Rowell)

Ellen Brown was a much loved Rehearsal Accompanist from 1972. During her time with the Society she married Charles Brown. Ellen was also a strong supporter of the Godalming Music Festival. She was given the honour of conducting our Summer Concert at Clandon House in 1985. The following is an extract from our programme for that concert.

TWO BY TWO

Clandon House, Guildford, 8th June 1985.

A Special Note for a Special Person

Ellen Brown has been our accompanist for the past twelve years, during which time she has won the hearts of all the members by her musical ability, hard work, constant help, endless patience and kindness.

It is with much regret that we have to announce that this is her last official appearance with us before retiring. As a mark of the esteem in which she is held, she was invited by our Musical Director, Robin Wells, to exchange roles with him for this concert – a special occasion for us all.

The Brown Family

Charles Brown joined the Society in 1927 and played tenor roles from 1929 to 1951. His wife Rachel (whom he met in the Society) and his two sons *Walter* and *Robert* also joined. Walter played tenor leads from 1951 to 1956, during which time he married one of the leading sopranos, *Doreen Mears.*

Yvonne and Tony Budd

Yvonne first appeared as a chorus member in **The Yeomen of the Guard** in 1972. In 1977, as well as being in the chorus in **Utopia Limited**, she was our Wardrobe Mistress. Although Yvonne no longer sings in the chorus, she is an invaluable member of the Society's Front of House team and has been for several years. Her husband Tony joined us for **The Yeomen of the Guard** in 1999 playing the part of First Citizen. In 2007 he played the part of Mr. Blushington in **Utopia Limited**. Tony's most recent appearance was in the 2012 production of **The Pirates of Penzance**.

Mr and Mrs G.R. Burgess (Randolph Burgess)

Mr and Mrs Burgess were founder members. Mr Burgess was the first Chairman of the Society. Both performed principal roles in **The Yeomen of the Guard** in 1925. They also played principal roles in some of the other early productions.

H.D. Coates

Mr Coates was the Society's first Honorary Treasurer in 1925 and co-guarantor with Mr G.R. Burgess.

John Conry

John Conry was Stage Manager from 1992 to 2000.

Don Covey

Don Covey was Stage Manager from 1948 to 1960. He was succeeded by *John Blunt* who worked jointly with Derek Raper until 1964. (See page 68 for more information on Derek Raper.)

John and Eileen Daykin

In 1953 John was appointed Manager of the National Provincial Bank in Godalming. Both he and his wife Eileen joined the Society in the same year.

They both performed in the 1954 production of **The Gondoliers**. John played the part of Luiz and Eileen was in the chorus. John was elected to the committee in 1956 until 1968. He became the Society's first Business Manager in 1962 – a position he held for the next six years. John worked for the Society with constant good humour and kindness, always putting the Society's needs before his own, especially when he found himself confronted with the part of Luiz! John played a number of principal roles until 1966, but remained as our Business Manager until the 1967 production of **Iolanthe**.

Eileen performed in all the productions until 1965. In her final year she played the part of Mad Margaret in **Ruddigore**.

Sally Dewey

Sally has been with the Society since 1976 as our orchestra leader. Over the years she has done much to ensure that the orchestra maintains its high standards.

Harry Evans

Harry's first appearance was in 1985 in **Iolanthe**. His most recent appearance was in **Patience** in 2011. Sadly Harry, who is remembered for his wonderful sense of humour, died on 21st August 2012.

Dick Frost

Apart from performing Dick Frost succeeded *Gilbert Streeter* as Chairman in 1960. He remained in the role until 1972.

Peggy Cherry-Garrard

Peggy Cherry-Garrard was a violinist in the orchestra from 1926 until 1957. She was also a founder member of Godalming Music Festival. Miss Cherry-Garrard was the sister of Apsley Cherry-Garrard, who was one of the youngest members of Captain Robert Falcon Scott's British Antarctic Expedition 1910-1912.

Mr O.C. Goodridge

Mr Goodridge was the Society's Treasurer from 1926 to 1930.

Alan Gray

Alan Gray became our Front of House Manager in 1961 until the late 1970s. He was ably assisted by other friends and members including *Eva Cozens* and *Jack Leggatt*, both of whom had a long association with the Society.

Anne Gray

Anne's first appearance was in the chorus of **The Pirates of Penzance** in 1970. She appeared in many of our productions both as a principal and as a chorus member until 1985.During 1983 and 1984 Anne served on the committee. She was also in the chorus in **The Grand Duke** in 2001. In 2003 Anne was choreographer for **Princess Ida**, as well as appearing in the chorus. In 1999 and 2000 Anne was director for the summer productions. When we performed **Oh What a Lovely War** in 2001 she was choreographer. Anne was the first editor of our newsletter "The Peeper" in 1982. After living in Spain for a number of years, Anne returned to Godalming and was appointed to the committee in 2012 as our new Hon. Secretary.

James Grossmith

James Grossmith, who was a pupil of Geoffrey Ford, played in the orchestra at the Guildford performances of our 1992 production, **Princess Ida**. It is worth noting that James was a direct descendant of one of D'Oyly Carte's most famous performers, George Grossmith – whose first role was that of John Wellington Wells in **The Sorcerer** in 1877. George Grossmith even performed as a pianist at a Royal Command performance at Balmoral for Queen Victoria.

Diana Harding

See entry for Michael Harding in Chapter 7: "Producers".

Sheila Harman

Before Sheila and her family moved to Devon she was our principal contralto, first appearing as Lady Blanche in **Princess Ida** in 1971, and finally as Queen of the Fairies in **Iolanthe** in 1976. More recently Sheila visited us in Godalming to give Master Classes.

The Hart Family

The following is an extract from Betty Moat's article for the Savoyard magazine at the time of our Golden Jubilee in 1975:

"Another family which merits special mention is the Hart family. Mr & Mrs Cecil Hart joined the Society in 1926 and were soon active committee members. Mr Hart played a number of principal parts between 1927 and 1939 and Mrs Hart was secretary from 1939 to 1959. Their son, Basil, joined in 1931 and married Mary Armstrong whom he met in the Society. Their son and daughter, Michael and Ann (Ing) were members during the sixties. Mr & Mrs Cecil Hart's daughter, Betty, also joined the Society, where she met her husband, Geoffrey Brown. Their membership extended into post-war years and their daughter, Daphne, was a member until she went to Australia. Basil and Betty's brother, Maurice, ran the Front of House activities before the war. When, as prisoner of war, he produced Gilbert and Sullivan in the prison camp. After the war ill-health prevented continuance of his work with the Society".

Barbara and Julian Hubble

Barbara and her son Julian joined the Society in the mid 1980s. Barbara's first performance was in **Iolanthe**, 1985 and Julian's in **Ruddigore**, 1986. Julian acts as Treasurer for the Social Committee and is involved in some of our behind the scenes work including the poster and leaflet distribution in various parts of Surrey. Barbara manages our rehearsal refreshment rota. Their most recent appearance was in our 2012 production of **The Pirates of Penzance**.

Janet and David Hughes

David first appeared in our production of **The Yeomen of the Guard** in 1980. Janet appeared for the first time in **Ruddigore** in 1984. Their most recent appearance was in **The Pirates of Penzance** in 2012. The publicity artwork for our production of **Ruddigore** in 2008 was designed by David.

Frederick Jeffrey

Frederick Jeffrey was born in Alresford in 1913. He lived a long life. Apart from his time with the Society, Fred was involved in many other activities. As a boy he became a member of the Scouts and he had a great deal of involvement with the movement. That continued when he moved to Rudgwick in the mid 1950s, initially running the local cub pack. Fred eventually became District Commissioner for the Horsham area. After he had stepped down from the role he, together with his wife Eileen, ran a Scout Shop every Saturday morning. Fred was also a very keen gardener and was successful in exhibiting at many horticultural shows.

After the Second World War, Fred pursued a career in aviation and joined Hawker Siddeley, which was later to become British Aerospace. He was appointed Airfield Manager at Dunsfold. One of his tasks was to placate local farmers who were not happy about the noisy jet fighters. In Fred's own inimitable style, and being very keen on cricket, he arranged matches between the local farmers and test pilots, as well as inviting them to hospitality events at the Farnborough Airshow. Prior to his career in civil aviation, Fred joined the RAF in 1939. Colour blindness prevented him from flying duties, so he worked as a member of the ground and maintenance crew. Part of his time in the RAF was also spent in the Middle East.

In 1954 Godalming Operatic Society beckoned and Fred's first performance was in the chorus of **H.M.S. Pinafore** in 1955. He continued until 1980: his last appearance was in **Princess Ida**. In the years that Fred was with the Society he also played a number of principal roles. From 1959 to 1962 he served on the Committee and was Chairman from 1972 to 1981.

In the late 1980s Eileen and Fred moved to Marnhull in Dorset. After moving Fred continued to enjoy gardening and had continued success in exhibiting at the local horticultural shows.

In 2009 Fred died at the age of 95. Michael Hartnall, our President, was invited to give an address at Fred's funeral. The information I have written above is from that very touching address. It is clear that Fred was a much loved and a well-respected member of the Society.

Rose Keen LRAM
Rose Keen was a founder member and rehearsal accompanist until 1930. Miss Keen was also a founder member of the Godalming Music Festival.

The Lucas Family
In this chapter mention has been made of family membership throughout the long history of the Society. It is worthy of note that, for our 2012 production of **The Pirates of Penzance**, just over 10% of the cast (representing three generations) were from one family. Peter Lucas, our Treasurer, was joined on stage by his father Antony, his mother Gillian, his sister Rebecca, and, making her first appearance with the Society, Peter's daughter, Hannah.

Alexander Lyon
Alexander (Leo) has been looking after our lighting design for many years. He is always on hand to set up the lighting rigs for the shows and effectively manages the stage illumination.

Geraldine Melhuish MBE
Gerry has been wardrobe mistress since 1989. In addition, Gerry and her late husband Peter, were presented with awards for their services to the disabled and for fostering disabled children since 1977.

Mr and Mrs C.E. Moat
Mr and Mrs Moat were founder members and performed in the 1925 production of **The Yeomen of the Guard**. Mrs Moat (Helen) was Mistress of the Robes for many of our productions and her association with the Society continued until the 1950s. Their daughter Betty became a member of the Society in 1938.

Betty Moat
See Chapter 3: "A Special Recognition".

Jennie Monk
Jennie Monk joined the Society in 1963. She played the title role in **Patience** in 1964, before becoming our accompanist from 1969 to 1973.

Jill Mussett
Jill was one of our Front of House Managers and was with the Society from 2000 to 2010.

Joan Nightingale (née Kerr)
Joan Nightingale designed and made the ladies' costumes for the 1967 production of **Iolanthe**. The practice of making the ladies' costumes continued for a number of years. The idea of making the costumes followed on from the success in 1957 by **Marjorie Bird.** Joan was our Wardrobe Mistress from 1970 to 1976 and she also designed the ladies' costumes for the 1976 production of **Iolanthe**. Her future husband **Peter** was a chorus member and our Business Manager. He also managed the cast's make-up.

Jill O'Regan

Jill returned to the Society in 2010 as Stage Manager for **The Yeomen of the Guard**. She was Stage Manager from 1978 to 1980 and again in 1982. Jill was also a Stage Crew member in 1983 and 1984. She stage managed our most recent productions: **Patience** in 2011 and **The Pirates of Penzance** in 2012.

Brian Oxborough

Brian was Front of House Manager from 1977 to 1999. For many years he worked with his wife Pat and brother John.

Mike Payne

Mike has had a long association with the Society as an occasional performer. He has also been very much involved with back stage – most recently for **The Pirates of Penzance** in 2012.

Jean and Keith Pratt

Although Jean is featured in Chapter 3: "A Special Recognition", her husband Keith was also a stalwart of the Society. More information about Keith is also included in Chapter 3.

Derek Raper

Derek Raper assumed total responsibility for Stage Management in 1964. As the role of stage management grew and as the Society expanded, it began to design and produce its own scenery; this was done between 1970 and 1974. Derek's mother, Brenda Raper, played the role of Gianetta in **The Gondoliers** in 1947.

Barbara Saunders (née Simm)

Barbara's first appearance was in the chorus in **H.M.S. Pinafore** in 1968 and more recently, in our 2011 production of **Patience**. Additionally, in 2012, she joined the cast for the Buxton performance of **The Pirates of Penzance**. During her 40 plus years with the Society, Barbara has undertaken principal roles from time to time. For many years Barbara has also been part of the Social Committee.

Herbert Shindler

Herbert Shindler was a founder member. As well as a performer, Herbert was also a Producer and a Stage Manager in 1925. In 1928 he performed in and directed **The Pirates of Penzance**.

Eileen Skelton LRAM

Eileen Skelton joined the Society in 1931 and was an active member both on stage and on the committee. She was assistant accompanist in 1932 and in the 1950s. In 1960 Eileen succeeded *Mrs Gilbert Streeter* as rehearsal accompanist until 1969. Eileen's parents also sold tickets for our shows at their shop in Bridge Street, Godalming.

Sheila and Charles Smith

During the 1980s Sheila and Charles Smith worked predominantly behind the scenes. Sheila was in the chorus for three productions between 1982 and 1989. She was also a Stage Crew member from 1985 to 1987 and looked after properties in 1988 and 1989. Charles was our Assistant Stage Manager in 1982 and Stage Manager from 1983 to 1989.

Sue Starbuck

Sue was Chairman for the 2001, 2002 and 2003 productions. She has performed with the Society on numerous occasions and has taken many principal roles. Her name first appears in the programme for the 1995 production of **Iolanthe**. Sue is one of our registered chaperones and currently is responsible for our make-up.

Violet Streeter

Violet Streeter was the first person to appear on stage for the Society playing the part of Phoebe in **The Yeomen of the Guard** in 1925. In 1935 Violet married *Kenneth Roberts*, who had joined the Society in 1929. After the Second World War they both continued playing principal roles. Kenneth was also the Society's Treasurer for 13 years. Violet and Kenneth were both appointed Life Members of the Society. In 1961, owing to Kenneth's work commitments, they moved to Hailsham. Violet's sister "Bing" (Randall) played mezzo-soprano and soprano roles until 1939. In 1975 Violet and Kenneth returned to Godalming for the Society's Golden Jubilee celebrations.

Gilbert A. Streeter MBE MC & Bar, Italian Silver Medal for Valour, JP

Mr Streeter (who was Violet's brother) had a long association with the Society from 1926 until 1969. Apart from performing, Mr Streeter had in turn, been Secretary from 1928 to 1935 (with a two-year break in between), Chairman from 1946 to 1960, Vice-President from 1961 to 1966; and President from 1967 to 1969 (See Chapter 16: "Presidents"). Mr Streeter died on 28th March 1992 at the age of 96.

(Note: The Italian Silver Medal for Valour is a WW1 award; it is the equivalent of the British Military Cross).

Mrs Gilbert A. Streeter LRAM

Mrs Streeter, or Day Streeter as she was known, was also a member of the Society from 1926 until 1969. Initially she was Assistant Accompanist before becoming Rehearsal Accompanist from 1930 to 1960. After 1960 Mrs Streeter continued to assist accompanying until 1969. As with the other members of her family, she too was actively involved with the Godalming Music Festival.

Christine Streeter

Christine, who was the daughter of Mr and Mrs Gilbert Streeter, joined the Society in 1946. She was in the 1947 production of **The Gondoliers**. Christine also had a long and illustrious career with the Society, performing many principal roles. Christine, like other members of the family, was very much associated with the Godalming Music Festival and was its Secretary from 1955 to 1970.

Sue Tilling (née Hilborne)

Sue is a valuable chorus member. Her first performance was in **The Mikado** in 1974 and her most recent appearance was in **The Pirates of Penzance** in 2012. Sue has also been an active member of the Social Committee

Ralph Truckle

Ralph Truckle (who was born in Peperharow Road, Godalming on 1st January 1905) decided he wanted to be a violinist from about the age of nine. His parents were told to contact a young lady, Miss Daisy (Day) Fay. Miss Fay (who married *Gilbert Streeter*) later became the Society's accompanist. She recommended Ralph to Miss Annis Mounsey, a violinist, who agreed to take him on as a pupil.

Ralph's first public appearance was with Miss Mounsey at Godalming Parish Church of SS Peter and Paul. They played Bach's Double Violin Concerto. Ralph subsequently studied at the Guildford School of Music. From the age of 16 he was a member of a trio playing for silent films at a cinema in Guildford. He also played at many other venues in the locality. When silent films were superseded by 'talkies', Ralph was then without regular employment, so he freelanced at many events.

In 1947, after the interruption of the Second World War, Ralph started to play violin again. He played for the Society for the first time in 1948. He was in the orchestra until our Golden Jubilee year in 1975 and was Leader from 1957. Ralph was also a member of the Charterhouse Orchestra.

Years later Ralph enjoyed his "retirement" as an ad-hoc assistant in the music department at Charterhouse from 1970 to 1981. Unfortunately, during the last few years of his life, he discontinued playing because his sight was deteriorating, resulting in complete blindness.

Ralph was appointed Life Member at the 1976 AGM. Robin Wells endorsed the proposal saying that "he was one of the last amateurs; a player very great to have on one's left-hand side, where he always did a very good job".

Ralph died on 25th September 1999. As a tribute to him, The Godalming Music Festival has a trophy in Ralph Truckle's name for the String competition.

I am grateful to Janice Maskell, Ralph's daughter, for the information that she provided about her father.

Anne Wainwright
Anne helped and managed our Front of House team for 30 years until 1997. To mark her retirement a special presentation was made to Anne at the AGM in 1998.

John Weeks
John Weeks made his first appearance in **The Sorcerer** in 1966 when he played the part of Alexis. He appeared on a number of occasions until 1980, playing mostly principal roles. John served on the committee in 1977. For a number of years until his death on 30th March 2012, John was a member of Godalming Choral Society.

Phyllis Western
Phyllis Western joined the Society in 1946 and was Hon. Secretary from 1959 to 1969. Her husband Dennis was also a member.

Rolf Whicker
Rolf Whicker was the Headmaster of Hillside School. He was a new member in 1947 playing many bass parts. Rolf worked continually for the Society until his death in 1969. His son Michael was a chorus member.

Irene Wright
Irene is a Matron and a Housemaster's wife at Charterhouse. In addition to being choreographer for the Society, she has produced our Summer Concerts in recent years. Irene was born in Edinburgh and started dancing at the age of 2 ½ years. She appeared in many professional productions as a dancer, including the world famous White Heather Club. Irene was also a director of the Ben Travers Theatre from 2000 to 2004. Her husband David, in addition to his role at Charterhouse, is the musical director of the Godalming Band.

CURRENT LIFE MEMBERS

Ambrose Barber

Ambrose has been a member since 1973. His last performance was in our 2012 production of **The Pirates of Penzance**. Ambrose co-wrote the one-act operetta **A Frank Affair**, which was performed at our Summer Concert in 2008. He was Chairman from 1998 to 2000.

Alan Browning

Alan, who plays flute in the orchestra, has been with the Society since 1964. Our 2013 production will be his 50th show.

William Llewellyn MBE B.Mus. FRAM ARCO

See Chapter 6: "Musical Directors".

John Mackney

John performed in the chorus for many years from 1974 until 2002: his last performance being **The Gondoliers**. He was our Business Manager from 1978 to 1980. John later served as a committee member from 1992 to 1994 and was Chairman from 1994 to 1997.

Jean Pratt

See Chapter 3: "A Special Recognition".

Linda and Michael Scanlon

Linda's first show was in the chorus of **Princess Ida** in 1982. Michael's first appearance was five years earlier in 1977, in our first production of **Utopia Limited**. Linda (apart from performing in the chorus) has managed the Society's Box Office for many years. She also compiles the programme for our annual G&S productions. Michael (apart from being a chorus member) has been the Society's Business Manager since 1985.

More details about the Box Office, Programme compilation and Business Management can be found in the Chapter 14: "How it All Works".

Hammy Sparks

See Chapter 7: "Producers".

Christopher Wheeler

Chris was an outstanding master at Charterhouse where he taught French and German. He played bassoon and was a member of the orchestra from 1976 to 2006. Chris and his wife Ann (who was an Archivist at the school) were also members of Godalming Choral Society for many years. They now live in Cumbria.

CHAPTER 10
THE ORCHESTRAS AND ACCOMPANISTS

THE ORCHESTRA 2010

What a wonderful air of expectancy must have been felt in Godalming Borough Hall at 8.00pm on Thursday, 15th February 1925 for our first G&S production and our first orchestra. Eighteen musicians, under the baton of Dr A.A. Mackintosh, our first musical director, play the overture for **The Yeomen of the Guard.**

And from the opening bars of the overture:

Allegro brillante e maestoso.

(Lively, sparkling and majestic).

After the overture the stage curtains opened to reveal Phoebe, played by Violet Streeter, at her spinning wheel, to begin what was to become the lively, sparkling and majestic story of Godalming Operatic Society.

As a Society we are very proud of the fact that today, for all our main G&S productions, we enjoy the accompaniment of a full orchestra of at least 22 musicians. Performing with an orchestra means that our audiences have the benefit of seeing and listening to performances of the highest quality in their traditional and purest form. There is no doubt that the orchestra lifts the standard and provides an essential support for our shows.

In our early days the concertina and the piano formed part of the orchestra. The use of the piano continued when we resumed productions in 1947 up until 1970.

Looking back to the 1870s there were 31 musicians in Sullivan's pit orchestra. Apart from the string section, the rest of the orchestra comprised of 2 flutes, 1 oboe, 2 clarinets, 1 bassoon, 2 horns, 2 cornets, 2 trombones and a percussionist. The number of musicians was increased by two for **The Yeomen of the Guard** in 1888, when a second bassoon and a bass trombone were added. Today the Society's smaller orchestra is traditional and similar in its set up. Of our 22 musicians we usually have 1 flute, 1 oboe, 2 clarinets, 1 bassoon, 1 horn, 2 trumpets, 1 trombone and a percussionist, with the string section making up the remainder. For some of our productions we have one or two additional musicians in the orchestra.

Our musical director undertakes the task of engaging the services of our musicians – some professional and some amateur. Many of our musicians have performed with the Society for a great number of years. For life member Alan Browning, flautist, our 2013 production will be his 50th show. More information about some of the individual members of our orchestras will be found in Chapter 9: "Personalities and Performers".

Before any of our shows reach the stage there is much rehearsal work to be done; and this could not be achieved without the support of an accompanist.

For our first production in 1925 the accompanist was *Miss Rose Keen LRAM*. Miss Keen was a founder member of the Society and continued as rehearsal accompanist until 1930. More information about Miss Keen and some of our other long-standing accompanists can be found in Chapter 9: "Personalities and Performers".

CHAPTER 11
CHARTERHOUSE

CHARTERHOUSE

A great deal of importance has to be placed upon our long and invaluable association with Charterhouse. The relationship between Charterhouse and Godalming (and especially to the Society) is an excellent example of "town and gown".

From the outset, the Society's first President, *Philip C Fletcher*, was a Housemaster at the school. He was Mayor of Godalming, and also had an active role in the Society as a performer. In the Society's early years Mr Fletcher's wife was a violinist and leader of the orchestra.

All our musical directors since 1926 were from Charterhouse. They have done much to ensure that the people of Godalming can enjoy the musical events that take place each year in the town. Apart from the contribution made by the musical directors, we must not forget that many other fine musicians from Charterhouse have also played their part in establishing such a rich heritage.

As a Society we have also benefitted by having talented people from Charterhouse as performers for our annual G&S production. They have also participated in production and choreography.

Prior to World War Two, some of our annual G&S productions were first performed in Charterhouse Hall and then at Godalming Borough Hall. Even when productions resumed in 1947, it was customary for pupils at Charterhouse to attend performances at the Borough Hall. In fact, in those days, there were two "opening" nights. The first night was entirely for the Charterhouse pupils and the second night for the public. On the 'Charterhouse pupil night' there was always additional audience reaction when one of the masters appeared on stage!

The immense support and vast contribution from Charterhouse to the town cannot be underestimated. In the Society's early years we were especially grateful for this support. We also enjoyed the use of the Llewellyn Room before eventually moving to a larger rehearsal venue.

CHAPTER 12
GODALMING MUSIC FESTIVAL

This book would not be complete without mentioning the long association that the Society has maintained with the Godalming Music Festival. In fact all the Society's Musical Directors have been involved with the Festival since 1947. At that time, *Arthur Trew*, our Musical Director, together with *Miss Rose Keen*, who was an accompanist, and *Miss Peggy Cherry-Garrard*, who played violin for the Society's orchestra, all attended the first meeting about the development of the Festival.

Since the inception of the Festival all our Musical Directors have had very significant roles in its organisation. *David Stone* our former Musical Director, is an Honorary President of the Festival, as is *Robin Wells* our current Musical Director.

In the early years the Society was very much involved in the Festival and also successfully competed. The Festival was held in early May to avoid clashing with our annual G&S productions in February. Nowadays, the dates of both the Festival and our production are close together which makes it difficult to participate in the Festival as a group. (The change of dates, however, enabled us to develop our Summer Concerts). Some of our members do enter individual events in the competition. In the Chapter 9: "Performers and Personalities" more can be found about some of the Society's members long association with the Festival. For example, The Streeter family, in particular, had a deep and lasting involvement with both the Society and the Festival.

I would like to mention one amusing anecdote associated with the Festival concerning a well-known local singer, Miss Jean Gaff, who sang as a soloist for both the Godalming Operatic Society and the Guildford Musical Society. The adjudicator declared that "both soloists were really excellent." When he was told that they were the same singer, Mr Roberton, the Adjudicator, remarked "Ah, a quick transfer. How much was the fee?" The Jean Gaff referred to is, of course, our newly appointed Vice-President, Jean Pratt.

More about the Festival and its connections with the Society can be found on the Festival Website: www.godalmingmusicfestival.org.uk

GOS MEMBERS DISPLAYING TROPHIES FROM THE 2010 GODALMING MUSIC FESTIVAL

Godalming Music Festival

CLASSES IN
MUSIC SPEECH DRAMA DANCE
&
MUSICAL THEATRE

Programme 2012
£2.50

25 February to 27 March 2012
www.godalmingmusicfestival.org.uk

CHAPTER 13
VENUES AND FINANCE

In this chapter I have included details of the various venues we have used over the years. In order to stage our productions financial considerations are an important factor. The second part of this chapter includes details of our need to sustain our income.

VENUES

Of all the main venues we have performed in, Godalming Borough Hall has always been our "home" theatre since 1925.

GODALMING BOROUGH HALL

Prior to 1939 some of our annual G&S productions were also performed at Charterhouse Hall before we opened at the Borough Hall. As stated in Chapter 11: "Charterhouse", pupils from the school attended the first night at the Borough Hall

In 1949 we gave the first of many performances in Guildford: our first show was **Iolanthe** at Guildford Technical College on Saturday 26th February. By performing at the college, we wanted to raise funds to donate to Farncombe Church Centenary Fund. We performed at the College until 1973.

In 1974 Guildford Civic Hall became our "second home" when we performed **The Mikado**. It remained our second home until 2003. Apart from our productions of the G&S operas, we performed at the Civic Hall on many other occasions. The Civic Hall had a very wide and high proscenium, but a rather shallow stage. Unfortunately, it was not ideal for G&S productions and dressing the stage was a nightmare.

The closure of the Civic Hall in Guildford presented a challenge to the Society; finding another venue suitable for our G&S shows proved to be difficult. Eventually we moved a bit further afield and selected The Leatherhead Theatre. Many people will remember this as the Thorndike Theatre. We opened there in 2004 with **The Mikado**. Although we were comparatively unknown in the Leatherhead area, we have gradually built up excellent audience attendances. We will perform our 10th production at the Leatherhead Theatre in 2013.

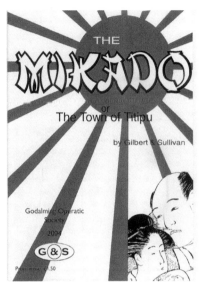

LEATHERHEAD THEATRE AUDITORIUM

THE MIKADO WAS OUR FIRST SHOW AT LEATHERHEAD

Among other venues that have frequently been used by the Society are Clandon House and The Electric Theatre in Guildford. Both of these venues have been used primarily for our Summer Concerts. Our first visit to Clandon House was in 1983 where performances took place in the Marble Hall. Unfortunately access to the hall was not permitted until after the last visitors to the stately home had departed which left little time to prepare for the concert. Also the ante-room used by the cast had to be treated with the utmost respect: they could only place personal items/props in certain places and then with great care. It is perhaps not surprising that the title of that Summer Concert was **Upstairs, Downstairs**!

In 1997 we presented our first Summer Concert at The Electric Theatre. We performed **Hiawatha's Wedding Feast** and the one-act operetta **The Batsman's Bride**.

In Chapter 5: "Other Productions and Summer Concerts" you will find listed other venues that have been used by the Society.

REHEARSAL VENUES

It has always been essential to have suitable rehearsal venues and we have been fortunate enough to have received excellent cooperation in this respect.

We currently rehearse at Moss Lane Primary School in Godalming. The central location of the school and its facilities has made it an ideal venue.

Rehearsal venues have also included the Llewellyn Room at Charterhouse and Godalming Borough Hall. To a lesser extent we have also used The Friends Meeting House, the Methodist Church (now the United Reform Church) and the Angel Lounge in Godalming.

FINANCE

The Society became registered as a charity in February 1990 with the clear objective of:

"Promoting public interest in the knowledge of the works of
W.S Gilbert and Arthur Sullivan".

Before World War Two, costs of staging the annual production were solely met by member subscriptions, ticket sales and contributions made by Patrons.

After the war rising costs made it necessary to increase the Society's income. One of the problems was the limited seating capacity at Godalming Borough Hall. The seating comprised 300 uncomfortable chairs. After much lobbying of local councillors by our then Chairman, Michael Hartnall, in the 1980s, Waverley Borough Council purchased new raised seating. There was a dramatic improvement in comfort and sight lines for the audience; but unfortunately, the seating capacity was reduced to 235.

Before the new seating was installed at the Borough Hall, additional income was needed. In 1949 we staged two performances at Guildford Technical College which had nearly 600 seats. After five months of rehearsing, our members were keen to give additional performances to benefit the Society.

In 1973, when the Technical College became unavailable, we moved to the Civic Hall in Guildford. This move was not without a huge amount of trepidation as the hall held 1,000 seats. Despite the staging difficulties, Guildford became our principal source of income for 30 years.

After the Civic Hall closed we then moved to The Leatherhead Theatre. The theatre proved to be a near perfect facility, with a capacity of 475 seats. The income derived from our performances at Leatherhead is essential to the on-going viability of the Society.

The cost of mounting our annual G&S production is substantial. Very often two sets of scenery and costumes are needed. The scenery has to be adaptable to the larger stage at Leatherhead as well. In addition, there is the cost of venue hire and the services of a 22 piece orchestra. Other costs include publicity, printing, music stand hire and lighting.

Despite the high costs, as a Society, we are committed to performing the full canon of the G&S operas. You will see that, apart from **Thespis**, we have lived up to our commitment.

Apart from our own promotions, the annual G&S production and our Summer Concerts, the Society is frequently asked to appear in other concert venues. In these instances, the Society would not be the promoter because it would not take the financial risk. On some occasions soloists or small groups appear at various events, but not the whole company. Some of the concerts listed in Chapter 5: "Other Productions and Summer Concerts" were not solely promoted by the Society.

CHAPTER 14
HOW IT ALL WORKS

As with many other organisations, the business of planning and preparing for our productions can be complex. Perhaps surprisingly, the management team consists of a fairly small committee who attend only six or seven formal committee meetings during the course of a year. The various officers of the committee have clearly defined roles and they are required to set, and to keep, the wheels in motion for the next production.

The Annual General Meeting of the Society usually takes place in June. Apart from the business of an AGM, it is at that time when all members of the existing committee step down. They can of course be nominated, like other members for election to the committee, for the ensuing year. All committee members are Trustees of the Society.

During the course of the AGM the outgoing committee recommends to the Members their suggestion for the next G&S production. At the same time, ideas are sought for a theme for our next Summer Concert.

The selection of our next G&S production is essential at an early stage. We need to be aware of what other the societies in the area are planning, in order to avoid the same show being presented locally at, or around, the same time. It is partly for this reason, that we do not perform the shows in strict rotation. Also, we like to intersperse one of the lesser performed operas from time to time.

Before describing in more detail of "How it all Works", it is worth mentioning here what the objectives of the Society are:

OUR OBJECTIVES
- To produce the best amateur productions of all the Gilbert and Sullivan operas as is possible within the Society's resources, including the use of a full orchestra.
- To provide a friendly and enjoyable Society that is inclusive of all age groups and ability.
- To seek ways to promote the works of Gilbert and Sullivan to younger generations.
- To be known as a Society that specialises in the works of Gilbert and Sullivan and attempt to produce all their works, both popular and rarely performed.
- To provide our members with the opportunity to develop their skills in the performing arts.
- To work in partnership with other dramatic societies, local authorities and community groups – the aim being to educate our community in the pleasures of the Savoy Operas.
- To endeavour to support the arts by entering various competitions, musical events and by supporting other societies that strive to promote the works of Gilbert and Sullivan.

CHAIRMAN

The Chairman is the focal point for all our members. His/her role is to keep a steady hand on the tiller and to liaise with and advise other members of the committee. He/she also is responsible for ensuring that the Society's image is maintained to a high standard.

HONORARY SECRETARY

The Hon. Secretary has a varied role. Apart from the task of recording the minutes of committee meetings, the Hon. Secretary has many other important tasks to perform. He/she manages our rehearsals and auditions in conjunction with the producer and the musical director. He/she is also responsible for keeping members up-to-date with the rehearsal schedules.

HONORARY TREASURER

Another important cog in the wheel is the Treasurer who not only ensures that the bills are paid on time, but is also responsible for ensuring that other fees such as insurance and membership subscriptions to other organisations are kept up-to-date. There is, of course, the important need to finalise our annual accounts for audit. Once the accounts have been approved, they are presented at the AGM giving members an opportunity to see how we have performed, in the financial sense, in comparison with previous productions.

HONORARY MEMBERSHIP SECRETARY

The Membership secretary is invariably the first point of contact for potential new members. One of his/her tasks is to keep membership records up-to-date. He/she also ensures that each member has a copy of the Society's rules. He/she is also responsible for the collection of membership fees.

BUSINESS MANAGEMENT

On the business management side it is essential to ensure that venues are booked. Arrangements need to be made for the hire of sets and scenery, as well as costumes. Acquisition of the stage sets can involve quite a bit of travelling for the Business Manager; also we have to bear in mind that performing at two different venues means that the sets need to be adaptable because of the varying stage sizes. In addition, there is a need to obtain and to make props as required by the Producer. Liaison with the theatres is very important to ensure that we have the right facilities. We also have to demonstrate that we have a sound Health and Safety Policy in place. Transport also needs to be arranged to move the sets from Godalming to Leatherhead. The Business Manager is responsible for co-ordinating the "get-in" at the theatres and checking that everything is collected after the run has ended.

HONORARY PUBLICITY OFFICER

Publicity for the upcoming production starts at quite an early stage. Some of the publications we use have very long lead times. One of the tasks that the Publicity Officer does is to liaise with other committee members regarding the poster and leaflet design. Once the design and layout is agreed, arrangements can be made for printing. As we get closer to the production date, it is necessary to keep in touch with various media outlets and to obtain as much publicity as possible. This includes updating quite a number of entertainment websites. In some instances we pay to advertise in local publications. Early in the New Year the hard work of poster display and leaflet distribution takes place in earnest. There is also a need to attract new members so a short "recruitment" campaign is usually run during the summer.

HONORARY PATRONS SECRETARY

The Hon. Patrons Secretary maintains the register of people who support the Society as Patrons. At the time of our production (before tickets go on general sale) our Patrons are contacted so that they can take advantage of our priority booking scheme.

THE COMMITTEE

Apart from the Officers' roles the other committee members have many important functions too – such as maintaining our website. Within the committee there are small working sub-groups: one which looks after the preparation of our newsletter "The Peeper". Another example is where a small working group prepared and co-ordinated matters for our production of **The Pirates of Penzance** in Buxton, August 2012. The Committee is also responsible for the appointment of the Musical Director and the Producer.

YOUNG MEMBERS AND CHILD PROTECTION

The Society welcomes young people who are interested in singing and performing on stage. Each G&S production provides a wonderful opportunity to develop performing art skills from rehearsals to the actual production. There is also the benefit of professional music direction and accomplished stage direction, as well as being accompanied by a full orchestra.

The Society, as required by legislation, has a Child Protection Policy in place. One of our committee members serves as our Child Protection Officer; and the policy is periodically reviewed to ensure that the requirements are adhered to.

ARCHIVE

The Society is extremely proud of its comprehensive archive, which is maintained by our newly appointed Vice-President, Jean Pratt.

WEBSITE

It seems appropriate to mention some information that can be found on our well-maintained website. The most important and interesting section is the Gallery. Here you will find details of our G&S productions since 1925, including cast lists and many excellent photographs. There is also information about our Box Office, becoming a Patron, becoming a member and who to contact. The website has a section for members use as well. The address of the website is: **www.godalmingoperatic.org**

COMMUNICATION

A significant change in recent years is the introduction of email and the internet. We also publish a newsletter called "The Peeper", which Jean Pratt edited until 2009. When the newsletter was first published it was edited by *Anne Gray*.

At this stage we do not "Tweet", as we feel that when it comes to Twitter, that W.S. Gilbert was way ahead of us all when he wrote "Eagle high in cloudland soaring – Sparrow twitt'ring on a reed...." (**Utopia Limited**)!

THE SOCIAL SIDE

We are lucky to have a separate Social Committee who organise regular, varied and enjoyable social activities. For example: evening walks during the summer months, followed by drinks at a local pub, plus a wonderful garden party in July. At the start of the rehearsal season plans are underway for, maybe, a Barn Dance and, of course, there is our Christmas Party.

One of the traditional aspects of our shows is to have a meal between the Saturday matinee and the evening performance. A party is also arranged after the final performance at Godalming Borough Hall.

It was a different kettle of fish before World War Two. In those days the cast would adjourn to the Borough Hall Court Room for their meal; there being no "Meat or Fish" on the menu, members were provided with ham, tongue and salad – like it or not! In later years, baked potatoes were on the menu. On one memorable occasion, the heat that was generated from the kitchen (which was close to the stage) overwhelmed one of the cast members who was on stage; he fainted and needed to be supported until the curtain fell!

SUMMER WALKS AND BARN DANCES ARE TYPICAL OF EVENTS ORGANISED BY THE SOCIAL COMMITTEE

REHEARSALS

In mid-September rehearsals for our next G&S production get underway. The first six sessions are with our Musical Director. The main focus is on the chorus parts at this stage. We usually start on the first night with a complete run through of the score. In the following weeks we then study and learn our parts.

After the initial singing sessions the "floor" work with the producer begins. The usual format (until Christmas) is that the chorus rehearse on a Monday evening with the principals attending if required. The principals usually attend on Thursday evenings. In the New Year the full cast is required on both Monday and Thursday evenings until the shows commence. There are usually one or two Sunday rehearsals at the Borough Hall as well. All the above leads up to the final rehearsals at the Borough Hall just before the show, followed by the all-important Dress Rehearsal.

At Leatherhead there are two final rehearsals: one being a technical rehearsal, in order to adapt to the larger stage size, and the other a full Dress Rehearsal.

AUDITIONS

Auditions for principal roles usually take place in early October a couple of weeks after the music rehearsals have started. Potential principals are given their pieces in advance by the Secretary. Auditions for principal roles are open to anyone – even to non-members. The only stipulation is that if a non-member is selected, then he or she is required to join the Society. It is the aim of the auditioning committee to let the person know as soon as possible (either by email or by telephone) whether or not he/she has been successful.

THE BOX OFFICE

Our Box Office usually opens to the general public to buy tickets for our G&S production in mid-December after our Patrons have had the opportunity to book their tickets. Before tickets can go on sale, the ticket printing for Godalming Borough Hall needs to be done in accordance with the seat plan. In the case of The Leatherhead Theatre, close liaison is needed with the theatre box office in order to agree a balanced allocation to suit ticket sales locally. Seat prices are reviewed from time to time by the Committee.

PREPARING THE PROGRAMME

An essential role is to prepare the programme for sale at the performances. This is quite a complicated process, as apart from the cast and orchestra lists and information about the show, other items need to be included. Photographs of the principals and chorus also need to be taken and included. Our Patrons, if they wish, are listed in the programme. A lot of "fine-tuning" has to take place before the actual printing of the programme, including the essential task of proof reading. It is interesting to note that, from 1925 to 1965, the price of one of our programmes was just 6 old pence – 2.5 pence in today's money!

We welcome advertisements. Many local firms place adverts in our programmes which we appreciate, as they help to support the Society. In the early years many adverts portrayed a humorous message relating to the actual production. A particularly interesting record can be seen in our 1939 programme for **H.M.S. Pinafore** and **Trial by Jury**. Parts of the 1939 programme are reproduced below. Understandably, there was quite a difference between the 1939 programme and the much smaller one printed for our first post-war production in 1947.

**A SELECTION OF ADVERTS FOR LOCAL COMPANIES
(MOST LONG GONE) FROM THE 1939 PROGRAMME FOR
H.M.S. PINAFORE AND TRIAL BY JURY.**

THE PRODUCTION AND STAGE MANAGEMENT

Apart from the performing cast, there are numerous essential activities that take place to ensure that everything runs smoothly. At Godalming Borough Hall, lighting rigs need to be set up. This usually takes place two or three days before the Dress Rehearsal. The lighting at The Leatherhead Theatre may also need adjusting prior to our performances. The set needs to be put into position and the all-important props put in place so that they are easily accessible.

Costumes are usually collected by the chorus on the Friday preceding the first performance in Godalming. During this time any problems regarding fitting are usually resolved. The principals' costumes are available for collection prior to the chorus collecting theirs. Our Wardrobe Mistress is on hand during all the performances to make any last minute adjustments, or repairs.

The Stage Manager, or the Producer, usually gathers everyone on stage before curtain-up to give a last minute briefing and to check that any inappropriate items, such as wrist watches, are removed and that make-up is applied correctly. The Stage Manager is also the focal point for behind the scenes activity. Our Musical Director may point out any parts of the score that need particular attention. Two other essential tasks need to be taken care of: one is that the "Call Boy" ensures that cast members are in place for their entrances and the second is that the "Prompter" stands in the wings throughout every performance.

SUBSTITUTES

There have been occasions when performing our annual G&S productions in February that we have needed (due to illness) a substitute for a principal role. Finding a replacement is not easy as, ideally, we need to find someone who can join us with virtually no rehearsal.

In 2007 there was a situation where the shoe was on the other foot. When we performed **Utopia Limited**, the same production was also being played later that year by the Peterborough Gilbert & Sullivan Players. Unfortunately one of their main principals was unwell, so one of our members, Richard Hales, stepped in at the 11th hour to perform the role of Captain Fitzbattleaxe in the Peterborough production.

CATERING

For every performance we need a team of people to provide refreshments for the cast and the orchestra in the "green-room". We fully appreciate the help we receive.

FRONT OF HOUSE

First impressions count. The Front of House team comprises a number of volunteers who are invaluable. A Front of House Manager ensures that the team greet people on arrival, so that they feel welcome.

THE WORK OF UNSUNG AND SOME UNSEEN HEROES.

In the first part of this chapter I described briefly how we manage a production from the early planning stages through to the final curtain. There are, however, numerous other tasks and many of our members, plus helpers, give their time and a great deal of effort to ensure that the shows are successful. The following list is an example of some of the tasks:

- Designing and printing of our advance booking leaflet and posters.
- Poster and leaflet distribution in the Godalming and Leatherhead areas.
- Hiring costumes for principals and chorus and arranging collection.
- For the production – some props need to be made.
- Transporting scenery and props between Godalming and Leatherhead.
- The "get-ins" at Godalming Borough Hall and The Leatherhead Theatre and the interval scenery changes.
- Returning costumes and removal of scenery and props at the end of the production run.

THE END

I hope the foregoing has given you an insight in to "How it All Works". By the time the final curtain falls at The Leatherhead Theatre, incredibly, more than 100 people will have been involved in bringing our annual G&S production to you.

WELL, NOT QUITE THE END........

After we have finished our two Saturday performances at Leatherhead, we think it is time for another party! Our hardworking Social Committee arrange this for the following day. After that we have a short break before rehearsals start again for our Summer Concert. It is true to say that the preparation for our Summer Concert is a lot less intensive than for our annual G&S production.

> ## *AND IT WOULD NOT WORK WITHOUT THE MOST IMPORTANT OF ALL....*

AUDIENCES

We have always been grateful for the loyal and wonderful audience support over the years. Each year we are delighted to see many familiar faces at Godalming Borough Hall and The Leatherhead Theatre. We are also pleased to be able to attract many newcomers to our productions. We know that many people travel great distances to attend our annual Gilbert and Sullivan production. Some people make the journey especially to see us when we are performing one of the rarely produced operas. Visitors to our shows are not confined to our shores either: one gentleman in particular, from the USA, always plans his annual visit to the UK in order to attend our G&S production.

CHAPTER 15
PATRONS

The Society has always welcomed Patrons, many of whom have attended countless performances. As we are a "not for profit" charity, the contribution made by our Patrons has always been greatly appreciated. The continued patronage is of significant importance and helps the Society to maintain high standards in its endeavour to preserve the works of Gilbert and Sullivan.

We feel it is important that our Patrons should benefit from their generous and continued support. As previously stated in the Box Office paragraph (page 83), one of the main benefits we offer Patrons is the opportunity to make priority bookings for our productions. In recent years we have had many occasions when our shows have been sold out well in advance, so priority booking has become worthwhile. Patrons also receive copies of our newsletter, "The Peeper" by email. The names of our Patrons are listed in the programme of our annual G&S production, unless they wish to remain anonymous.

When the Society was formed in 1925 the list of Patrons, compared to our current list, was quite short. The first list is reproduced here.

> **The 1925 List of Patrons**.
> Lt-Col. L. Benson, J.P.
> Sir Henry Buckingham, M.P.
> Dr and Mrs B.W. Bond.
> Major S.F. Chichester, J.P.
> The Rev. F.S. Colson.
> The Rt. Hon. Lord Daryinton.
> The Headmaster of Charterhouse
> and Mrs Fletcher.
> Lady Caroline Grenville.
> Sir Herbert and Lady Jekyll.
> E.J. Jeudwine, Esq.
> Edgar Horne, Esq.
> Dr and Mrs N.F. Kendall.
> The Earl and Countess of Midleton.
> Eric Parker, Esq.
> Lt-Col C. Parsons, D.S.O.
> The Rev. F. Pickford.
> Mrs G.F. Watts.

The list of Patrons from many of our other early productions can also be seen in the Gallery section of our website.

Footnotes

Sir Henry Buckingham was a Member of Parliament for Guildford.

The Headmaster at Charterhouse in 1925 was Mr Frank Fletcher, who was the cousin of our first President, Philip C Fletcher.

Lady Caroline Grenville was the daughter of the 3rd Duke of Buckingham and Chandos.

Sir Herbert Jekyll was Gertrude Jekyll's brother.

Lord Midleton was in the Cabinet in the early Edwardian days, at the India Office, Foreign Office. He was also Minister for Ireland.

Mrs G. F. Watts was the wife of the founder of Watts Gallery, George Frederic Watts.

The Rev. F.S. Colson, from the Parish Church of SS Peter and Paul, played the part of the Headsman in our 1925 production of **The Yeomen of the Guard**.

Chichester Hall in Witley opened in 1935. It was built in memory of Major Spencer Frederick Chichester.

> **If after reading the history of the Society, you would like to become a Patron,**
> **please refer to the Tickets section of our website for more details.**

CHAPTER 16
PRESIDENTS

In this chapter you will find details of most of the Society's Presidents since 1925. Regrettably, there are some gaps in the list from 1928 to 1930, when the name of the President of the day was not included in the programme, nor recorded in our archives.

The Society's first President in 1925 was the then Mayor of Godalming, *Philip Cawthorne Fletcher*. He was a Housemaster at Charterhouse and the cousin of the Headmaster Frank Fletcher.

Major Philip Cawthorne Fletcher MA MC TD JP (to give him his full title), had a long association with the Society. He became President again from 1931 to 1939. His wife Edith was a violinist and leader of the orchestra. As a note of interest, Major Fletcher, as the owner of the Broadwater Estate, presented four and a half acres of land to the Borough in 1937 to be used as a cricket ground.

In 1926 the President was the Mayor, *Cllr. W.F. Paine*. The Mayor, *Alderman Charles Burgess*, was President in 1927.

Cllr Mrs Dorothy C. Kirkcaldy was Mayor of Godalming in 1945. When the Society's productions resumed in 1947, she became President until 1956.

Major General R.L. Bond CB CBE DSO MC Hon FRAM was President from 1957 to 1966.

Gilbert A. Streeter MBE MC & Bar, Italian Silver Medal for Valour, JP, became President from 1967 to 1969. As stated in Chapter 9: "Personalities and Performers", Mr Streeter had a long association with the Society, together with his wife who, for many years, was our rehearsal accompanist.

William Llewellyn MBE B.Mus. FRAM ARCO became President in 1970 until 1991. More information about Mr Llewellyn (who was Musical Director from 1963 to 1968) can be found in Chapter 6: "Musical Directors".

Betty Moat BA LGSM see Chapter 3: "A Special Recognition".

Robin Wells FRCO GRSM ARCM Hon ARAM became Vice-President in 2005. For more information see Chapter 6: "Musical Directors".

Michael Hartnall FCA became the current President in 2006. His long association with the Society dates back to 1966 when he performed in a number of productions. Michael was also Treasurer from 1969 to 1977 and Chairman from 1981 to 1988.

Since he was a teenager Michael has had a passion for opera and gives lectures. On 16th March 2011, on behalf of Godalming Museum, Michael gave a fascinating talk in the Parish Church of SS Peter and Paul, entitled "Tales from Two Towns – The Gilbert and Sullivan Story in London and Godalming".

Mrs Jean Pratt – Vice-President. See Chapter 3: "A Special Recognition".

CHAPTER 17
THE SOCIETY NOW AND THE COMMITTEES

As a Society we think it is particularly significant that many of our predecessors would readily identify with our deep love of the works of Gilbert and Sullivan. On reflection, since 1925, the major change as to how we manage productions, has been the creation of the various ways that we communicate with each other: email, the Worldwide Web, etc. Other than that, and in our world of celebrating the works of G&S, little has changed. Long may it continue.

For any newcomer the opportunity to enjoy G&S in its purest form, either in the audience or as a performer, should not be missed. It is a wonderful experience and fun. Like many organisations we need to attract new members; therefore, we encourage people to participate in our shows. We welcome young people to join us. Performing on stage with a diverse and talented team is without equal. And the thrill of being accompanied by a live orchestra is incomparable. As mentioned in Chapter 14: "How it all Works", we have in place a child protection policy. It is worth mentioning here that two of our younger members **Hannah Crutcher** and **Katie Wood** performed in **H.M.S. Pinafore** at the Youth Festival at the International Gilbert & Sullivan Festival in Buxton in 2011. Katie won the award as the best female performer, which is an outstanding achievement.

An important element of the Society is that we are a registered charity. We maintain membership of various organisations such as NODA (National Operatic and Dramatic Association), GATA (Guildford Amateur Theatre Association) and Guildford Arts. We also maintain close contact with various other local organisations such as the Go Godalming Association.

Finally, one of the strongest attributes of the Society is the spirit of togetherness that exists between the members. While I was writing this book it became clear to me that such a spirit of camaraderie has been a common thread over the years. It has been a great privilege for me to have the opportunity to place on record the magnificent achievements of the Society. In many respects I feel that I have only skimmed the surface of the Society's long history. I am pleased to say that the **History of Godalming Operatic Society** is an unfinished story.............

THE COMMITTEES

In Chapter 14: "How it all Works", you will have read about the various roles of each of our Committee members. In other chapters you will also find references to the many people who, over the years, have volunteered their services as a committee member.

It is clear that much is owed to the committee members who, in the past, have done so much to bring the Society to what is today. In recognition of their contribution, it is essential that successive committees continue to maintain these well-founded traditions.

The following members formed the Committee for the year commencing June 2011. Their first G&S performances with the Society are also shown. Two of our long-standing main committee members: Chairman, Hammy Sparks and the Hon. Secretary, Jean Pratt, stood down at the time of the 2012 Annual General Meeting.

THE MAIN COMMITTEE 2011/2012

Chairman	**Hammy Sparks (Iolanthe,** 1976)
	(See also Chapter 7: Producers)
Hon. Secretary	**Jean Pratt (Princess Ida,** 1952)
	(See also Chapter 3: A Special Recognition)
Hon. Treasurer	**Peter Lucas (The Pirates of Penzance,** 2000)
Hon. Membership Secretary	**Jeff Holliday (Patience,** 1998)
Hon. Business Manager	**Michael Scanlon (Utopia Limited,** 1977)
	(See also Chapter 9: Personalities and Performers)
Hon. Publicity Officer	**Eddie Powlesland (The Sorcerer,** 2006)
Member (Editor "The Peeper")	**Chris Howard (The Sorcerer,** 2006)
Member (Webmaster)	**Piers Plummer (Utopia Limited,** 2007)
Member (Child Protection Officer)	**Nora Price (The Gondoliers,** 1991)

Richard Hales (Princess Ida, 2003) became the new Chairman for the year 2012/2013 and **Anne Gray (The Pirates of Penzance,**1970) - (see Chapter 9: "Personalities and Performers") was appointed as the new Hon. Secretary. The rest of the Main Committee remains unchanged.

THE SOCIAL COMMITTEE 2011/2012

As mentioned in Chapter 14: "How it all Works", the Society places high value upon the work that is carried out by its Social Committee. Many members have, over the years, put in a great deal of effort to ensure that apart from our shows there is much else to enjoy. For the year commencing June 2011 the following members formed our Social Committee. Their first G&S performances with the Society are also shown.

Chairman	**Alan Knight (Princess Ida,** 2003)
Treasurer	**Julian Hubble (Ruddigore,** 1986)
Member	**Helen McEvoy (Ruddigore,**2008)
Member	**Chris Howard** (see Main Committee)
Member	**Jeff Holliday** (see Main Committee)
Member	**Nathan Morley (Utopia Limited,** 2007)
Member	**Paul Tickner (Ruddigore,** 2008)

Additionally, Alan Knight's wife Sheila (**Princess Ida,** 2003) and Joan Robinson (**The Mikado,** 2004), were co-opted to the Social Committee and again for 2012/2013.

At the 2012 AGM, Elaine McGee (**Patience,** 2011) was elected to the Social Committee in place of Paul Tickner. However, Paul was co-opted to the committee for 2012/2013, as was Margaret Polydorou (**The Pirates of Penzance,** 2012) – stage management team.

CHAPTER 18
MILESTONES

The Society has celebrated many memorable events throughout its long history. Perhaps the most significant was its Golden Jubilee in 1975 and the celebration dinner that took place at The Hogs Back Hotel. The front cover and the toast list for the dinner are reproduced here.

19th February 1925	Our first ever performance: **The Yeomen of the Guard.**
5th February 1947	Our first production following WW2: **The Gondoliers.**
15th March 1947	First steering committee meeting for Godalming Music Festival.
26th February 1949	First performance in Guildford at the Technical College: **Iolanthe.**
15th February 1974	First performance at the Guildford Civic Hall: **The Mikado.**
20th March 1975	OUR GOLDEN JUBILEE YEAR. Celebrated with a special dinner at the Hogs Back Hotel.
19th September 1981	A concert version of **Patience** was performed to celebrate Godalming's centenary as being the first town in the world to have a public electricity supply.
7th May 1983	Our first Summer Concert: **Upstairs – Downstairs** at Clandon House.
20th February 2004	Our first performance at The Leatherhead Theatre: **The Mikado.**
22nd August 2005	Performed **Iolanthe** in the International G&S Festival Buxton Opera House.
24th September 2007	Performed **Utopia Limited** in the Waterford International Festival of Light Opera at the Theatre Royal.
20th February 2010	Robin Wells special presentation celebrating his 40 years as Musical Director after the evening performance of **The Yeomen of the Guard**, Godalming Borough Hall.
10th July 2011	Presented with the NODA "Accolade of Excellence" for our district for the 2011 production of **Patience.**
15th August 2012	Again at the International G&S Festival, Buxton Opera House, performing **The Pirates of Penzance.**

CHAPTER 19
G&S PRODUCTIONS SINCE 1925

THE YEOMEN OF THE GUARD (9)	1925, 1931,1951, 1961,1972,1980,1989,1999, 2010.
PRINCESS IDA (8)	1926,1935,1952,1960,1971,1982,1992,2003.
THE GONDOLIERS (9)	1927,1933.1947,1954,1962,1969,1979.1991,2002.
THE PIRATES OF PENZANCE (8)	1928,1936,1959,1970,1981,1990,2000,2012.
IOLANTHE (8)	1929,1949,1957,1967,1976,1985,1995,2005.
THE MIKADO (9)	1930,1937,1948,1956,1963,1974,1983,1993,2004.
PATIENCE (8)	1932,1938,1953,1964,1973,1987,1998, 2011.
RUDDIGORE (8	1934,1950,1958,1965,1975,1986,1996,2008.
HMS PINAFORE (7)	1939,1955,1968,1978,1988,1997,2009.
TRIAL BY JURY (as a companion piece) (6)	1939, 1955, 1966, 1978, 1988, 1997.
THE SORCERER (4)	1966,1984,1994,2006.
UTOPIA LIMITED (2)	1977, 2007.
THE GRAND DUKE (1)	2001.

IN ADDITION: Other curtain raisers as companion pieces were performed as follows:
Cox and Box in 1936 and 1990 and The Zoo in 1981.

The Zoo was performed as part of our Summer Concert in 2002, Cox and Box was performed in our Summer Concert in 2003 and Trial by Jury was performed in our Summer Concert in 2004.

THE ORIGINAL GILBERT AND SULLIVAN LONDON PERFORMANCES
FOLLOWED BY THE YEAR OF THE FIRST PERFORMANCES BY
GODALMING OPERATIC SOCIETY

Thespis 1871 - 63 performances	(not yet performed)
Trial by Jury 1875 - 131 performances	Godalming - 1939
The Sorcerer 1877 - 178 performances	Godalming - 1966
H.M.S. Pinafore 1878 - 571 performances	Godalming - 1939
The Pirates of Penzance 1879 - 363 performances	Godalming - 1928
Patience 1881 - 578 performances	Godalming - 1932
Iolanthe 1882 - 398 performances	Godalming - 1929
Princess Ida 1884 - 246 performances	Godalming - 1926
The Mikado 1885 - 672 performances	Godalming - 1930
Ruddigore 1887 - 288 performances	Godalming - 1934
The Yeomen of the Guard 1888 - 423 performances	Godalming - 1925
The Gondoliers 1889 - 554 performances	Godalming - 1927
Utopia Limited 1893 - 245 performances	Godalming - 1977
The Grand Duke 1896 - 123 performances	Godalming - 2001

To find out more about the Society
please visit our website:

www.godalmingoperatic.org

for details of

Forthcoming productions

~

Buying tickets

~

Becoming a Patron

~

Joining our mailing list

~

Taking part as a performer

~

Helping backstage

There is also a photo gallery with images of almost
every production since 1925, as well as programme
details from every year.

A set of "Cigarette Cards" featuring the principals from the
2010 production of *The Yeomen of the Guard*.

Made in the USA
Charleston, SC
21 December 2012